ISRAEL

AND THE HOLY LAND

PHOTOGRAPHS BY WERNER BRAUN
ILLUSTRATIONS BY WALTER FERGUSON
COVER ART BY HARRY McNAUGHT

A GOLDEN REGIONAL GUIDE

GOLDEN PRESS • NEW YORK

FOREWORD

This guide presents the many facets of the modern State of Israel, as well as the most important sites of the Holy Land both in Israel and in Jordan.

The lands of the Bible, of course, extend far beyond the State of Israel. The site of the Garden of Eden is, traditionally, in Mesopotamia (Iraq). Moses received the Ten Commandments on Mount Sinai between Egypt and Arabia. Nevertheless, most of the holiest places of both the Jewish and Christian faiths are within what was Palestine. The Old City of Jerusalem, where Solomon built his Temple, where Jesus was tried and condemned to die on the cross, and from which Mohammed is believed to have ascended to heaven, is close to the hearts of Christians, Jews, and Moslems.

We are grateful to the many people and organizations that have contributed to making this book possible. Among them are Drs. L. Fishelson and S. Helvig of the University of Tel Aviv; Drs. I. Harpaz, S.P. Monselise, Y. Shiloh, T. Yizraeli, Miss E. Werker, and Prof. H. Oppenheimer of the Hebrew University in Jerusalem; Dr. E. Mazor of the Weizmann Institute of Science; Dr. Samuel Terrien of Union Theological Seminary; Drs. E. and H. Boyko, Mr. J. Hoofien, the Rt. Hon. Viscount Samuel, and Dr. David Samuel. Also, to the Israel Government Press Office, the Israel Ministry of Religious Affairs, the Israel Tourist Corporation, and the Jordan Tourism Authority.

R.S.

Copyright 1967 by Western Publishing Company, Inc. All rights reserved, including the right of reproduction in whole or in part. Designed and produced by Les Editions des Deux Coqs d'Or, Paris, France. Printed in the U.S.A. by Western Printing and Lithographing Company. Published by Golden Press, Inc., New York, N.Y. Library of Congress Catalog Card Number: 67-29420.

AUTHOR'S NOTE

As this book goes to press (following the armed conflict which broke out between Israel and her Arab neighbors on June 5, 1967) no permanent solution has, as yet, been found to the problems which have harassed the Near East for the past twenty years.

At present, the entire area west of the Jordan River (which was once Mandated Palestine), the Sinai Peninsula and the Syrian plateau overlooking the Galilee, are under Israeli control. These, and all other significant changes, are indicated in the text.

R. S.
July, 1967

CONTENTS

ISRAEL is an independent republic, carved from Palestine and established in 1948 as the first ward of the United Nations. Israel proper, with 8,000 sq. miles, is about the size of the state of New Jersey.

Diversity is the most characteristic feature of Israel—diversity of people, of religions, of climate, of flowers, and of birds. The landscape is strikingly varied, with plains and mountains, lakes and seaboard, desolate hills and pleasant valleys, fertile fields and arid deserts, all within relatively short distances of each other.

Even more remarkable is the contrast in the customs of the people, who have come from all parts of the world. The present population is over 2½ million. Each in his own way is loyal to traditions ranging from those of Biblical days to those of the second half of the 20th century.

SABRA is fruit of cactus plant, prickly outside, sweet inside.

SABRA is now a term to designate Israeli-born Jew.

JERUSALEM, the Old City and its walls, seen from the terrace of King David Hotel in the New City.

Thousands of years of history have left their mark in the Holy Land and a wealth of tangible evidence connects it with mankind's past. Contemporary finds include human relics of more than 100,000 years ago; 10,000-year-old Jericho; Canaanite towns built 5,000 years ago, Roman theatres 2,000 years old, 12th century Crusader walls, and 18th century Turkish towers.

The annals of the Holy Land's antiquity are exciting, but so is the story of modern Israel. The challenge of a land poor in natural resources and the drive towards progress by her citizens have made this a land like no other today.

OLD RABBI is an immigrant from Yemen.

ARAB BOY is one of many Bedouin in Israel.

TIPS TO TOURISTS

Both Israel and Jordan are accessible by air, by sea, and by land. Visas are required for most nationalities, and can be obtained either through Israel or Jordanian consulates or your travel agent. Until June, 1967, crossing from Jordan into Israel was only possible in Jerusalem, through the Mandelbaum Gate. At present, arrangements to visit the holy places can easily be made in Israel. The borders between Israel and its Arab neighbors are currently closed to tourists, as they have been for many years.

A valid smallpox vaccine certificate is required.

The best time to visit Israel and most of the other lands of the Bible is spring, when the hills are green and wild flowers are in bloom. But the trip can be comfortable in all seasons: Summer is hot, but the brownness of the hills has its special charm, and summer nights are cool and starlit. The months from November to April are the rainy ones, but showers are followed by bright sunshine.

Light-weight clothing is most comfortable and appropriate. In Israel, dress is very casual: men wear open-collared sport shirts. Women can wear informal clothing, but should dress conservatively when visiting religious quarters and sites. A dark suit will suffice for any but the most formal occasion.

A warm sweater may be needed in the evening. A raincoat and rubbers are necessary in the winter—and flat-heeled walking shoes are a must.

ACCOMMODATIONS   Comfortable, even luxurious, hotels are available. In Israel, more than 200 hotels have been approved by the Tourist Corporation. In Jordan, most of them are small inn-type hotels. Deluxe accommodations are available to those who want them.

There are reasonably priced youth hostels affiliated with the International Youth Hostels Association. Christian visitors on a pilgrimage can stay in hospices.

A stay in a *kibbutz,* the collective community unique to Israel, is an interesting experience. Reservations should be made well in advance, particularly in summer. Lists of hotels, youth hostels, hospices, and *kibbutzim* are available through travel agencies.

SABBATH is a day of rest in Israel. Government offices, public places of entertainment, and shops are closed. On Saturdays, most transportation stops, and in some hotels only cold meals, ordered in advance, are served. Friday is the day of rest for Moslems; the tourist facilities in Jordan are unaffected, but the visiting of mosques should be avoided.

THE CURRENCY in Israel is the Israel pound (IL), divided into 100 agorot, and worth 33 U.S. cents. In Jordan, it is the dinar, divided into 1,000 fils, and worth $2.80.

GUIDES   It will be helpful, in visiting sites of the Holy Land, to take a guide to accompany you. Licensed guides are competent and knowledgeable. In Israel, he wears a golden lapel pin with the words "Licensed Tourist Guide." In Jordan, a guide may be asked to show his Tourism Authority License.

The official languages in Israel are Hebrew and Arabic, but many other languages are spoken, notably French, English, Yiddish, German, and Russian. In Jordan the language is Arabic, but English is widely used.

Reasonably priced, typical gifts are available, such as ceramic and leather goods, jewelry, rugs, fabrics, and sweaters in Israel; olive-wood bound Bibles, Bedouin jewelry and rugs, pottery, and glassware in Jordan. Antique collectors may come across interesting bargains in government-licensed shops.

A typical 10-day tour:

1st day: Arrival at Lod International Airport near Tel Aviv. Drive to Jerusalem.

2nd, 3rd and 4th days: Visit Jerusalem, including the Old City, the Mount of Olives, Gethsemane and Bethlehem. **(Extra day,** for which permission can be obtained in Israel: Bethany, Jericho, Qumran and Hebron. Return to Jerusalem.)

5th day: Visit Nazareth, Tabgha, Tiberias, the Galilee and Safad. Drive to Haifa.

6th day: Visit Haifa, Acre, Caesarea. Drive to Tel Aviv.

7th day: Visit Tel Aviv, Jaffa and surrounding area.

8th day: Drive to Beersheba and Eilat via Rehovoth.

9th day: Eilat: Solomon's Pillars. Glass-bottom boat or underwater exploration of coral reef in the Red Sea.

10th day: Drive to Masada, Herod's fortress, and the Dead Sea. Return to Tel Aviv.

(In Jordan: A two-day tour can be taken from Amman to Petra, 50 miles south of the Dead Sea, staying overnight in a "tent hotel" open from March 1 to May 31, and Sept. 1 to Oct. 31. Petra can only be reached on horseback from the "hotel," about 1½ hours each way.)

CALENDAR OF EVENTS

The Jewish era starts with the traditional creation of the world in the fall of B.C. 3761. The 354-day year has 12 months of 30 days; 7 leap years of 13 months each in a 19-year period make the length of the Jewish year average that of the solar year.

The Moslem era starts with the year of the Hegira,

Mohammed's flight from Mecca to Medina in A.D. 622. The year has 345 days made up of 12 lunar months. Moslem dates do not regularly correspond to standard dates: 33 Moslem years are approximately equal to 32 solar years.

The Eastern Orthodox churches follow the Julian calendar (named for Julius Caesar) which is 13 days behind the Gregorian calendar (named for 16th century Pope Gregory XIII) of the Roman Catholic and Protestant churches.

MAIN JEWISH HOLIDAYS

YOM KIPPUR The Day of Atonement, 10 days after Rosh Hashanah, the New Year. (Sept.-Oct.)

SUCCOTH The week-long Feast of the Tabernacles, five days later, recalls the booths lived in by the Israelites during their 40 years in the wilderness.

SIMHAT TORAH The Rejoicing in the Law on the last day of Succoth.

HANUKKAH The 8-day Feast of Lights (Nov.-Jan.) marking the victory of the Maccabees over the Greeks, and the rededication of the Temple in 164 B.C.

PURIM (Feb.-Mar.) commemorates 5th century B.C. Queen Esther, who saved her people from a Persian plot to destroy them.

PESACH Passover (Mar.-Apr.) recalls the Exodus of the Children of Israel from Egypt. Begins with the traditional Seder service on the first evening.

YOM HA'ATZMAUT Israel's Independence Day on the 5th of Iyar. (Apr.-May)

SHAVUOT Pentecost (May-June) celebrates the Festival of the First Fruits; also marks the giving of the Law.

MOSLEM HOLIDAYS

RAMADAN The 9th Moslem month during which fasting is required from dawn to sunset. It commemorates the revelation of the Koran.

ID AL FITR Three days of feasting marking the end of the Ramadan Fast.

ID AL ADHA Four-day feast of the Sacrifice commemorating the ransom of Abraham's son Ishmael with a ram.

MUHARRAM Mourning for the death of the Prophet's grandson, Husain.

CHRISTIAN HOLIDAYS

The dates for Easter and holidays connected with it vary from year to year as Easter is always the first Sunday following the full moon that falls on or after March 21.

GEOGRAPHY

ISRAEL lies on the eastern seaboard of the Mediterranean, along ancient and modern routes connecting Europe, Asia, and Africa. It is bounded by Lebanon and Syria in the north, Syria and Jordan in the east, and Egypt in the southwest.

Israel proper is 265 miles long and varies in width from 12 miles, north of Tel Aviv, to 70 miles, south of Beersheba, and only 6 miles at Eilat. The total area is 7,992 square miles, of which 172 are water. It is on the same latitude (29°-33° N) as the states of Georgia and Alabama. The northern half of Israel consists of successive parallel bands running north to south:

The Mediterranean beach with its white sand and occasional steep cliffs.

The coastal plain, with its cities and orange groves.

The central mountain spine which includes Galilee and Samaria, and the Judean and Hebron Mountain chains. Highest point in Israel is Mount Meron, also known as Mt. Atzmon, (3,692 ft.) in northern Galilee.

The Rift Valley, farther east, along which the Sea of Galilee, the Jordan River, the Dead Sea, and the Gulf of Eilat are located.

The Negev, Israel's southern half, a hilly to mountainous desert.

JUDEAN HILLS and fertile plain below

OLIVE TREES in southern coastal plain

THE CLIMATE of Israel is influenced by its location between the well-watered lands of the Mediterranean and the arid reaches of Africa and Asia. The weather in the Negev is like that of large stretches of the Sahara. In Galilee, it is similar to that of the north Mediterranean. The climate of Jerusalem resembles that of central Europe, while the coastal plain enjoys the typical warm summers and mild winters of the Italian Riviera. The one factor common to the whole country is the division into only two seasons—a dry summer and a rainy winter, which starts around November and ends in April. Between January and March, most of the year's rain pours down in sporadic torrents of several hours' duration, usually followed by sun. In spring and autumn, the hot, dust-laden easterly or southeasterly wind, the *Sharav*, from the Arabian desert, makes for a few trying days. It is a country of bright sunlight. In June the sun rises about 4 a.m., in December about 7 a.m.

THE RIVERS of Israel are few. The most important are the Yarkon, north of Tel Aviv, and the Kishon, near Haifa, both flowing from the central mountains to the Mediterranean. The most famous is the Jordan, which begins in Lebanon and Syria and flows due south.

ARID RED CANYON in the Negev on the way to Eilat

SANDY BEACH along the Mediterranean coast in Nathanya

MEDITERRANEAN SEA

LEBANON
Beirut (50 miles)
Tyre
Acre
Haifa
Athlit
Caesarea
Nathanya
TEL AVIV
Jaffa
Lod
Ramla
Rehovoth
Ashdod
Ein Karem
Ashkelon
Beit Guvrin
Gaza
Lachish

MT MERON
Safad
Tabgha
Nazareth
Tiberias
Megiddo
Jenin
Nablus

Hazor
Qnaitra
Damascus (20 miles)
Cheik Meskine
SYRIA

Sea of Galilee
Jordan
Irbid
Deraa
Salkhad
MT AJLUN
Mafraq
Jerash

Jericho
Qumran
Jerusalem
Bethlehem
Hebron
Dead sea
Ein Gedi
Masada
Beersheba
Dimona
Sdom
El Kerak

AMMAN
Qasr el Azraq
Qasr Mushatta
Madaba

SAUDI ARABIA

NEGEV

JORDAN

Avdat
Aba Aweiquila
Mitspe-Ramon
Rekhes Menuha
Petra
Ma'ān
Naqb el Ashtar

EGYPT
(SINAI PENINSULA)

Timna
Elat
Aqaba
Gulf of Aqaba

Note: Borders are shown as they were from 1957 to 1967.

LEGEND
- - - - Border
——— Roads
+++++ Railroad
——— Rivers

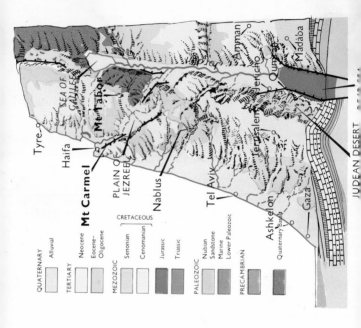

Map legend:

QUATERNARY — Alluvial

TERTIARY — Neocene; Eocene–Oligocene

MEZOZOIC — CRETACEOUS — Senonian; Cenomanian — Jurassic; Trassic

PALEOZOIC — Nubian Sandstone; Marine Lower Paleozoic

PRECAMBRIAN — Quaternary Basalt

Map labels: Tyre, SEA OF GALILEE, Mt Tabor, Haifa, Mt Carmel, PLAIN OF JEZREEL, Nablus, Tel Aviv, Ashkelon, Gaza, Jerusalem, Jericho, Amman, Madaba, Qumran, JUDEAN DESERT

GEOLOGY

All the major geological formations common to the Middle East are readily seen in Israel, due to the remarkable variety of the country's geological structure, and to its sparse soil coverage.

Outcrops of Precambrian rock—some of the most ancient parts of the earth's crust—are found near the Red Sea. The erosion of granite, syenite, gneiss, schist, and other bedrocks which are crossed by thousands of dikes (intrusions of molten rock into fissures of older rock), produced the rugged landscape of Eilat.

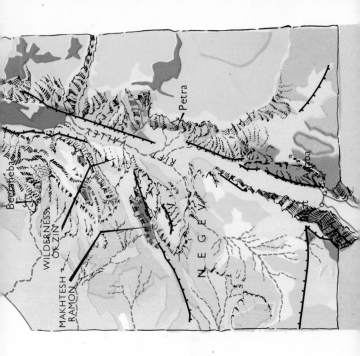

King Solomon's Pillars at Timna, north of Eilat, were
carved out of Paleozoic sandstone and conglomerate
by rain and wind. In some localities these rocks are still
covered with shales, rich in copper, which were deposited by an ancient sea. It was from this "Nubian" sandstone that King Solomon's slaves, and later Roman
prisoners, mined nodules of copper. The mine shafts
and slag heaps can still be seen. The seas of Triassic
and Jurassic time, advancing from the northwest, never
reached as far south as this.

MAKHTESH in the Negev. Remains of Roman encampment have been found atop its ridge.

KING SOLOMON'S PILLARS at Timna carved in Paleozoic sandstone by rain and wind

MAKHTESHIM   Outcrops of sedimentary rock deposited during the Triassic and Jurassic periods are vividly exposed in the Negev Makhteshim—large, bowl-shaped erosional depressions surrounded by steep cliffs up to 1,300 feet high. The Makhteshim take their name from the Hebrew word for grinding mortars. They resulted from complex erosion over millions of years. The three best-known Makhteshim are the round Makhtesh Katan (about 4 miles in diameter); the more elongated Makhtesh Gadol (9 miles long, 3 miles wide); the Makhtesh Ramon (25 miles long, average width 5 miles).

During the Lower Cretaceous Period sandstones were deposited in the south, shales and limestones to the north. In the latter strata oil has been found at Heletz, on the coastal road to Beersheba, and gas at Zohar, west of the Dead Sea. The Upper Cretaceous Era left deep sediments: limestone, chalk, marl, clay, dolomite, and flint. Out of these formations Israel's mountainous regions have been sculptured.

Mountain-building shifts of the earth's crust of the

MUSHROOM pillar of Nubian sandstone, shaped by rain and windblown sand

CHALK ROCKS of Rosh Hanikra on Mediterranean seashore near Lebanese border

Tertiary Period are responsible—along with erosion—for the present-day relief. Some crustal blocks were heaved up; others sank. A chain of sunken blocks forms the famous Rift Valley. The Jordan River, the Sea of Galilee, the Dead Sea, and the Gulf of Eilat all lie in basins of the Rift. The Arava Valley is another such basin. During the rainy Pleistocene Epoch all or most of the depressions were filled with fresh water. Today most of these lakes are salt or dry.

In Quaternary times the swamps of the Huleh, at the head of the Jordan Valley, were formed by lava flows that blocked the upper course of the Jordan. The Lisan Lake, most famous of the Pleistocene fresh-water lakes, shrank, becoming the fresh-water Sea of Galilee and the highly saline Dead Sea. Many hot and mineral springs developed in the Rift Valley during the Quaternary; among them are those at Tiberias, on the Sea of Galilee, and Hamei Zohar, on the Dead Sea. It was in the Quaternary that the present outline of Israel's coastal plain on the Mediterranean was formed.

NATURAL HISTORY

PLANTS OF THE HOLY LAND The outstanding feature of the Holy Land's plant life is its variety. Vegetation ranges all the way from that typical of the Mediterranean—as in the hill regions and along the coastal plain—to the lush tropical plants of the Jordan Valley, and the hardy desert shrubs of the deep Negev. There are some 2,500 species of plants, including over 200 mentioned in the Bible. The medicinal herbs and wild flowers of the Holy Land are famous. The crocus and the meadow saffron appear right after the first rains and are followed by a carpet of other flowers, including the hyacinth and cyclamen. Fruit trees begin to bloom in January. Indigenous trees include the Jerusalem pine, the tamarisk, and the carob which, with the imported eucalyptus, are widely used for afforestation in Israel. Citrus groves today cover more than 100,000 acres.

TREES OF THE BIBLE Trees are frequently referred to in the Bible. These are six of many of these trees which still grow in the Holy Land today:

Olea europea

OLIVE is one of the first trees mentioned in the Bible. It can reach 25 ft. Olive wood was used to decorate the Temple doors and is still used ornamentally. The fruit, harvested at the beginning of the autumn, is used for food and oil. Grows mainly in hilly regions.

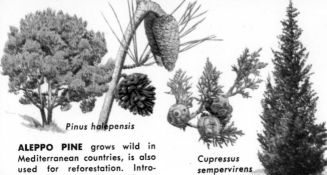

Pinus halepensis

ALEPPO PINE grows wild in Mediterranean countries, is also used for reforestation. Introduced from Lebanon, not Aleppo (Syria). Up to 60 ft.

Cupressus sempervirens

CYPRESS up to 80 ft. high, grows mostly in hills. Used largely as an ornamental tree and as windbreak in orange groves. Its wood was used in shipbuilding by Phoenicians, Greeks and Romans.

Quercus calliprinos

CALLIPRINOS OAK, up to 40 ft., can also look like small shrub if grown on dry soil. It is commonest tree in Holy Land, chiefly in its dwarf form.

GREEN BAY TREE or Laurel, Biblical emblem of wealth, can be a shrub or tree. Broken evergreen leaves emit strong scent, used as spice.

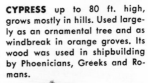

Phoenix dactylifera

DATE PALM (up to 100 ft.) has 6 ft. leaves, no branches. In Biblical times it supplied food, fuel, clothing and was used in triumphal processions.

Laurus nobilis

19

BIBLICAL FRUITS

Vitis vinifera

GRAPE is the cultivated plant most often referred to in the Old Testament. When Moses sent scouts to explore "the Promised Land," they returned with the grape of Eshkol, a branch with a single cluster so large they had to carry it on a pole. Many grapes now grow on terraces in hilly regions.

Prunus communis (Amygdalis)

Prunus armeniaca

ALMOND (up to 25 ft.) is the first tree to flower in the year. Pink or white blossoms appear before leaves. Nuts were used for oil and ointments.

APRICOT (up to 30 ft.) one of the Holy Land's popular fruits; unknown in Palestine before first century B.C. It has pale rose flowers with dark red centers.

FIG (up to 30 ft.) is one of the first plants mentioned by name in the Bible. Flowers are enclosed in hollow container and fertilized by fig wasp.

POMEGRANATE (up to 20 ft.) has clear, red, juicy seeds inside a thick jacket. The juice was a favorite beverage and its flowers were used medicinally.

Ficus carica

Punica granatum

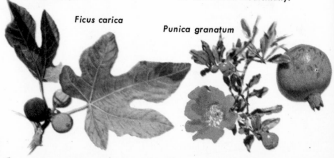

Commiphora opobalsamum

BALSAM (up to 15 ft.) is believed to have been brought to Solomon from Ethiopia by the Queen of Sheba. "Balm," used for perfume and medicine, is from the resin of the tree.

Coriandrum sativum

CORIANDER (1 to 3 ft.) an umbelliferous plant with leaves like parsley, belongs to the carrot family. Seeds and leaves were used to flavor food.

Myrtus communis

MYRTLE (3 to 10 ft.) prized for its fragrant leaves and scented flowers, is still collected during the Feast of Tabernacles and woven into a ritual wand.

FLAX (up to 36 in.) the most ancient of all known textile fibers. Textile is produced from the stem, oil from seeds.

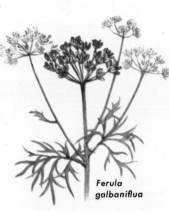

Ferula galbaniflua

GALBANUM, the juice of the *Ferula galbaniflua,* a strong-rooted perennial with small greenish-white flowers, was burned as incense in the Temple. With aloe, myrrh, frankincense, cassia, cinnamon, and olive, it made the holy oil to anoint officiating priests.

Linum usitatissimum

21

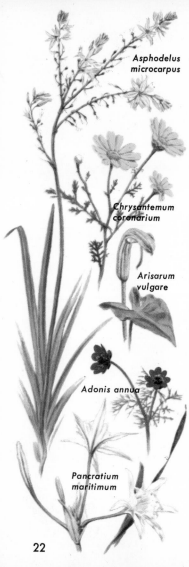

Asphodelus microcarpus

Chrysantemum coronarium

Arisarum vulgare

Adonis annua

Pancratium maritimum

TALL ASPHODEL (3 ft.). A perennial, dormant in the summer, can be seen over much of the Holy Land in late winter and early spring. It is a member of the lily family. Roots contain starch from which gums and alcohol were made in ancient times.

COMMON CHRYSANTHEMUM (2 to 3 ft.) is found throughout Israel and adjoining areas in dense masses, often taking over entire fields and roadsides. Brilliant gold flowers appear in March and April.

JACK IN THE PULPIT or Friar's Cowl, a perennial which grows in shady places in early winter, can be spotted by the greenish striped sheath encasing the flowers which grow on a thick stalk. Arab peasants use the flowers to heal bruises and wounds.

PHEASANT'S EYE (15 in.) blossoms late in the procession of red spring flowers. Insects attracted by bright color, as flower lacks scent and nectar. Known in medicine for alkaloid adonin, similar in effect to digitalis. Grows in coastal plain, Judean Hills, and Mount Carmel.

SEA PANCRATIUM (10 in.) one of the handsomest flowers of the coastal plain, blooms in late summer before the first rains. The strongly scented white flowers, which open in the evening, precede the long and spearlike leaves.

EVENING PRIMROSE (1 to 2 ft.), introduced from the U.S., is found along the coastal plains where its roots go deep in the sand. Flowers bloom at the height of summer and open toward evening. Its leaves are covered with hairs which prevent evaporation.

ANISE FENNEL (3 ft.) is a high bushlike herb flowering in midsummer. Deep taproots bring up water and leaves are so finely dissected that there is little evaporation. In moist places, it grows large juicy leaves. The fruit is used as a spice.

PALESTINE IRIS (10 in.). Unlike Israel's many other irises, grows low and spreads. Leaves are thick. Grows throughout much of the Holy Land. Its Greek name *iris* has been in use since Hellenistic times.

NAPLES GARLIC (1 ft.) is one of the most common and beautiful of the *Allium* species in Israel. Grows in hilly regions and on the coastal plain. Leaves are flat and hairless.

PERSIAN CYCLAMEN (6 to 8 in.) is one of the Holy Land's most popular wild flowers. Likes rocky shade in the Judean Hills and in Galilee. Flowers from January to April.

Oenothera biennis

Foeniculum piperitum

Iris palaestina

Allium neapolitanum

Cyclamen persicum

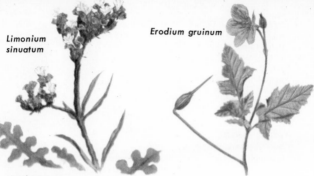

Limonium sinuatum

Erodium gruinum

SINUOUS SEA LAVENDER (up to 2 ft.) blooms from March to July, mostly on the coast. Its tough roots reach down for water below crumbly rock.

ITALIAN ALKANET (3 to 4 ft.) also called Ox-tongue from the shape of its rough leaves. It blooms in early summer throughout the Holy Land.

CRANE'S BILL (8 in.) an annual geranium with violet-blue petals whose color deepens during the day. When dry, seeds spiral round on a thin stem.

ANEMONE (12 in.), below center, grows all over the Holy Land in all shades of red, white, blue and purple. On rainy days the blossoms remain closed.

DWARF CHICORY (2 to 3 ft.) blooms in summer but its fine soft leaves sprout in the middle of winter. Arabs use it for salad. Flowers close by afternoon.

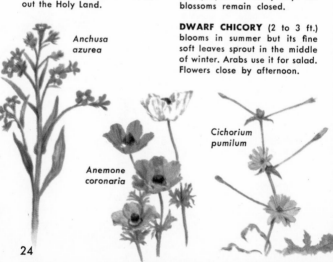

Anchusa azurea

Anemone coronaria

Cichorium pumilum

24

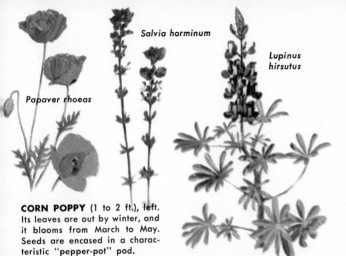

Salvia horminum

Lupinus hirsutus

Papaver rhoeas

CORN POPPY (1 to 2 ft.), left. Its leaves are out by winter, and it blooms from March to May. Seeds are encased in a characteristic "pepper-pot" pod.

PURPLE TOPPED SAGE, top center, is of the mint family. Its scented leaves attract insects. Can either remain low and thin, or grow tall and spread.

SYRIAN CORNFLOWER (1 ft.) blooms from February to May. One of Israel's blue flowers. Related species grow in cornfields throughout Europe.

HIRSUTE LUPIN (to 2 ft.). Leaves fold up at dusk. Its bitter seeds are poisonous; root nodules enrich the soil with nitrogen. Grows in the coastal plain.

FRAGRANT NARCISSUS (to 18 in.) appears throughout the Holy Land in November after the first rains. The strap-shaped leaves funnel moisture to the roots.

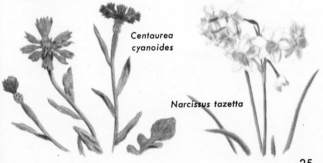

Centaurea cyanoides

Narcissus tazetta

25

DESERT VEGETATION

Acacia raddiana

Zizyphus spina-Christi

UMBRELLA ACACIA (20 to 25 ft.) is the most characteristic tree of the African savannah and its northernmost location is the Negev. A member of the mimosa family.

SAXAWL TREE (10 to 12 ft.), a true desert tree, lives for several hundred years. It furnished fuel for smelting in King Solomon's mines at Timna.

CHRIST'S THORN (10 to 15 ft.) is easily recognized by white twigs and tiny yellowish-green flowers. Its small orange-colored fruit is edible.

RETAM or White Broom, desert shrub common in wadis, has spread to coast where it stabilizes sand. Fragrant flowers look like snow. Bulldozed and burned, it is growing scarce.

Haloxylon persicum

Retama raetama

Limonium (statice) thouinii

Artemisia herba alba

LAVENDER (10 to 15 in., but up to 2 ft. thick stem) is found on salt and dry rock south of Dead Sea. Flowers from white to pink to purple.

WHITE WORMWOOD (10 in.) flowers in winter chiefly in central Negev. Leaves and branches contain refreshingly scented oil.

Iris mariae

Aaronsohnia faktorowski

MARIA'S IRIS (12 in.) endemic to sandy soil of the central Negev, is one of Israel's most beautiful plants. Blooms in spring.

AARONSOHNIA (4 in.) is a composite shrub common around Dead Sea and deep Negev. It lives for only a month or two, in the spring.

JOINTED ANABASIS is a poisonous desert succulent. In late summer has white and purple fruit.

SDOM APPLE (3 to 5 ft.) Ripe fruit bursts to release seeds. Beer can be made with leaves, a kind of rubber with sap.

Anabasis articulata

Solanum incanum

FLOWERS OF JERUSALEM AND OF THE CARMEL

Some of the Holy Land flowers, though they can grow in many parts of Israel and Jordan, are associated with special sites. Such are the flowers of Jerusalem, on this page, and of the Carmel, on the next.

Colchium steveni

Starnbergia spaffordium

STEVEN'S MEADOW SAFFRON (4 in.) appears the day after the year's first rain. Arabs call this crocus the "rain signal."

SPAFFORD'S STERNBERGIA (6 in.) blooms in autumn, its flowers opening each morning and closing at night.

SILVERY PLUMELESS THISTLE One of the 25 local species of thistle, this grows mainly on roadsides, ancient quarries, and in neglected places.

Carduus argentatus

GRAPE HYACINTH (6 in.). Long-stalked flowers on top are sterile. Larger flowers below along the stem are fertile and change color from purple to green.

Muscari (Leopoldia) comosa

STEMLESS HOLLYHOCK is the most common of many local hollyhocks. Flowers growing close to the ground bloom in spring. Other varieties often reach a height of 9 ft.

Ornithogalum eigii

SHORT-SPIKED STAR OF BETHLEHEM (8 in.). Easy to spot in the hills all spring. Larger varieties grow in the heavy soil of the plains.

Althaea acaulis

Ricotia lunaria

Ranunculus asiaticus

PRETTY CARMELITE (10 in.). Petals arranged like cross of the Knights of St. John. Blooms in spring until midsummer.

TURBAN BUTTERCUP (10 in.) is a perennial spring flower appearing in February, joined a few weeks later by poppies.

MARITIME SQUILL (3 ft.) blooms in August and September. The bulb contains substance used to treat heart disease.

Urginea maritima

Hyoscyamus aureus

Orchis papilionaceus

GOLDEN HENBANE hangs down from rocks and walls all over Holy Land. May have served as model for headdress of ancient high priests.

BUTTERFLY ORCHID (8 in.) or Carmel Orchid is common in the Holy Land. Stalks rise between downpours.

SUN'S EYE TULIP (14 in.). A showy scarlet flower of the hill regions, whose long narrow leaves are first seen in early winter.

VILLOUS ROCKROSE (up to 3 ft.) covers stretches of Mt. Carmel. Blooms February to May. Petals open in the morning, wither at night.

Tulipa oculus solis

Cistus villosus

29

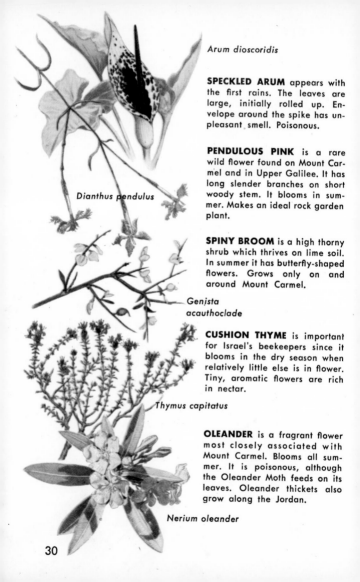

Arum dioscoridis

SPECKLED ARUM appears with the first rains. The leaves are large, initially rolled up. Envelope around the spike has unpleasant smell. Poisonous.

Dianthus pendulus

PENDULOUS PINK is a rare wild flower found on Mount Carmel and in Upper Galilee. It has long slender branches on short woody stem. It blooms in summer. Makes an ideal rock garden plant.

SPINY BROOM is a high thorny shrub which thrives on lime soil. In summer it has butterfly-shaped flowers. Grows only on and around Mount Carmel.

Genista acauthoclade

CUSHION THYME is important for Israel's beekeepers since it blooms in the dry season when relatively little else is in flower. Tiny, aromatic flowers are rich in nectar.

Thymus capitatus

OLEANDER is a fragrant flower most closely associated with Mount Carmel. Blooms all summer. It is poisonous, although the Oleander Moth feeds on its leaves. Oleander thickets also grow along the Jordan.

Nerium oleander

FISH OF THE HOLY LAND

About 300 species of fish have been identified in Holy Land waters. Among them are Mediterranean and Atlantic fish, many tropical Red Sea fish, and freshwater fish in the Sea of Galilee. No fish, of course, can survive the high mineral content of the Dead Sea. Carp, the most widely eaten fish in the area, is bred in artificial ponds. Inshore and pelagic fishing (for fish that live near the surface) is centered along the Mediterranean coast and at Eilat on the Red Sea. Most of the trawling is done in the Red Sea. The little tuna (sometimes called bonito) is found in the Red Sea. The sole is known in Hebrew as "Moses our teacher" because, according to legend, when Moses parted the Red Sea, he also split this fish in two. The halves later rejoined, but still can be easily divided. Two of the most typical freshwater fishes of the Holy Land are pictured below. They are found in the Sea of Galilee.

CATFISH (up to 4¼ lbs., up to 27 in.) is smooth and scaleless with broad head and fine teeth in bands. Transverse mouth is surrounded by whisker barbels. Takes a variety of food including insects. When caught, it sometimes squeaks like a kitten.

ST. PETER'S FISH (up to 4½ lbs. and 15 in.). Belongs to the cichlid family whose adult males and females keep the young in their mouths until they can manage alone. Traditionally, the fish St. Peter was eating when he learned that Jesus was risen.

Clarias lazera

Tilapia galilea

31

CORAL REEF FISH OF THE RED SEA

People, oil, and the shipping industry may one day eliminate tropical fish, still one of the attractions in the Red Sea. Meanwhile, many are still to be seen, by skin divers and visitors aboard glass-bottom boats.

The shallow waters glimmer with brilliant fish that live in colorful coral formations of varied shape, while deeper parts of the gulf abound with sharks, hammerfish, sawfish, and other large fish. Since the opening of the Suez Canal, many tropical fishes have entered the Mediterranean, and some species have acclimatized to the lower temperature.

1 SQUIRREL FISH (5 in.) or Soldier Fish is timid by day and active by night. Large preopercular spine can inflict wound when fish is handled.

Holocentrus

2 IMPERIAL ANGELFISH (15 in.). One of several angelfishes, and one of the most beautiful of all the reef fishes in the Gulf. Young are almost black.

Pomacanthus imperator

3 FIRE FISH (10 to 13 in.). Poisonous spines in dorsal fin. Feeds on smaller fish. When moving, its indented fins may have the appearance of flames.

Pterois volitans

4 MORAY EEL has thick skin, very small gill opening, and no pectoral fin. Snout is pointed and has numerous sharp teeth. Largest is about 5 feet long.

Gymnothorax

5 SMOOTH FLUTE MOUTH (4 to 5 ft.) has elongated fleshy body and a pronounced tube-like snout with mouth at the end.

Fistularia

6 PORCUPINE FISH (20 to 25 in.). Short body with dark blue or brownish spots covered with long spines which inflate (as in picture) when in danger. Yellow fins.

Diodon hystrix

7 BOXFISH (18 in.). Encased in an armor or hexagonal plates which fuse into a solid box. Slow, feeds mainly on small invertebrates.

Ostracion

8 BUTTERFLY FISH (8 to 10 in.) is the most common and most vivid tropical fish in the reefs of the Red Sea. Has compressed body and fine bristle-like teeth.

Chaetodon lunula

REPTILES Eighty-two species of reptiles have been found in Israel: 40 lizards, 34 snakes, of which seven are poisonous, and 8 turtles. All of these reptiles are carnivorous except the tortoises, and all egg-laying except the sand boa and some of the skinks which bear live young.

STARRED AGAMA (11 in.) is common in the north. Other species are more widespread. Male has two rows of scales on belly.

Agama stellio

DESERT MONITOR (to 4 ft.) lives in Negev and near Dead Sea. Eats mice, lizards, and snakes.

Varanus griseus

Chamaeleo chamaeleon

CHAMELEON (to 14 in.) changes color with change of environment. Eyes move independently.

Chalcides ocellatus

EYED SKINK (to 9 in.) lives mostly underground. One local species has no legs.

Hemidactylus turcicus

TURKISH GECKO (to 5 in.), commonest of 10 local species. Cling to walls.

Lacerta trilineata

SYRIAN GREEN LIZARD (15 in. and more). Found in the north, often in remnants of oak forests.

MOORISH TORTOISE (to 10 in.). A docile, vegetarian pet, with club feet. Digs in for winter.

Clemmys caspica

RIVER TURTLE (to 8 in.), or Caspian terrapin, can be seen on river banks, near ponds and marshes.

Testudo graeca

Typhlops vermicularis

GREEK BLIND SNAKE (to 12 in.). Almost blind, lives underground. Head (left) looks like tail.

Natrix tesselatus

DICED WATER SNAKE (3½ ft.). Increasing in number because of irrigation. Eats fish, frogs.

Vipera palaestinae

PALESTINIAN VIPER (to 4 ft.). Bite can be fatal. Often found north of Beersheba, and along coast.

Walterinnesia aegyptia

BLACK COBRA (3 ft.). Sometimes found south of the Dead Sea, is related to Indian Cobra. Poisonous.

Coluber jugularis syriacus

SYRIAN BLACK SNAKE (7½ ft.) is largest in Holy Land. Moves rapidly, eats mice, birds.

Eryx jaculus

JAVELIN SAND BOA (to 28 in.) is dwarf member of boa family. Kills prey by constriction.

MONTPELLIER SNAKE (to 7 ft.) is found on coastal plain, even in built-up areas.

Malpolon monspessulanus

Camelus dromedarius

ARABIAN CAMEL (7 to 8 ft. high at the hump). Popularly known as the dromedary, it provides the Bedouin with transportation, milk, meat, and wool, and its dung is burnt for fuel. Lives on desert vegetation and can do without water for as long as a week. A riding camel can travel over 100 miles a day.

MAMMALS

Although the lion, the hippopotamus, and the elephant have long been extinct in the Holy Land, wolves and leopards can sometimes still be found in Galilee and in the desert. Occasionally, the honey badger can be seen in the Negev and in parts of the Jordan Valley. The mongoose still roams in the coastal plain and in the northern part of Jordan. The camel can be seen at every Bedouin encampment. All together, there are some 70 species of mammals. Most are smallish, nocturnal, and can go without water for long periods. Some of those commonly seen are described below.

Sus scrofa libycus

WILD BOAR (3 to 5 ft. long). Now facing extinction, it lives mainly in what is left of the Huleh swamps. Like all pigs, it is omnivorous. The male uses his curved tusks to battle his rivals. A nocturnal animal, it relies on extra-sharp sense of smell to lead it to food.

NUBIAN IBEX (40 to 60 in. long, height 33 in.). Lives in herds near the Dead Sea and in the desert where it finds water. The female is smaller and beardless. Herds can sometimes be seen walking in single file behind a leader. A sure-footed mountain-climber, it can jump as high as 7 ft. Has keen eyesight and sense of smell.

ARABIAN GAZELLE (about 3½ ft. long, tail 4 in., height 2½ ft.). Grayish-brown or grayish-yellow, depending on surroundings. Sharp sight and hearing. Lives in rocky areas and thickets. The female has shorter, thinner horns. A southern species, the Dorcas gazelle (2 ft. high) is lighter in color, has long ears, and lyreshaped horns.

STRIPED HYENA (about 3 ft. long, tail 15 in.) can be found in hilly areas. Its short, weak hind legs prevent it from pouncing on live prey and it feeds largely on carrion or on dying animals, but will kill domestic stock. Massive teeth and jaws for crushing bone; dorsal crest of long hair. Howl has often been mistaken for laughter. Is nocturnal and has poor sight.

WOLF (about 3½ ft. long, tail 15 in.). Though common to the Holy Land during Biblical times, it is now seen rarely—near the Dead Sea, in northern Galilee or in Southern Arava. Feeds on deer, small domestic animals, also on mice, insects, and some fruit. Those found in the south are lighter in color and smaller.

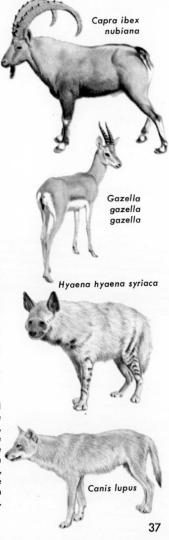

Capra ibex nubiana

Gazella gazella gazella

Hyaena hyaena syriaca

Canis lupus

37

Canis aureus syriacus

Herpestes ichneumon ichneumon

SYRIAN JACKAL (2½ to 3½ ft. long, tail 12 to 17 in.). Looks like small wolf. Seen all over the Holy Land, particularly near inhabited areas where it finds its food: small animals, birds, carrion, also grapes and melons. Has an eerie high-pitched shriek. Mainly nocturnal. Notorius carrier of rabies.

EGYPTIAN MONGOOSE, OR ICHNEUMON, (up to 2 ft. long) was sacred in ancient Egypt. Lives in hedges and among rocks. Preys on birds, eggs, mice, snakes, lizards. Disliked by farmers because it is destructive to poultry (and mentioned as such in the Talmud). Mother and young have a characteristic "Unk unk" call.

SYRIAN HYRAX, known in the Bible as Cony, (up to 20 in. long) lives in colonies of up to 50 in rocky cliffs or hilltop boulders chiefly near the Dead Sea, the Carmel range, and northern Galilee. Although rabbit-sized, it is more closely related to the elephant and the rhinoceros.

Procavia capensis syriaca

Hystrix indica

INDIAN CRESTED PORCUPINE (about 30 in. long). Holy Land's largest rodent. Widespread except in sandy areas of the south. Has a hairy muzzle and crest of long white bristles. Lives in caves and burrows. Erects its black and white quills and rattles its tail when frightened. Feeds on roots and fruit.

EGYPTIAN FRUIT BAT (4 to 5 in. long). One of Israel's largest bats, with a wing span of 14 to 18 inches. Lives on fruit (figs, mulberries, peaches). Has a shrill squeak. There are more than 20 species of small insect-eating bats, mostly in caves near the Dead Sea, the Jordan Valley, and the Sea of Galilee.

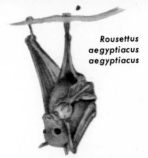

Rousettus aegyptiacus aegyptiacus

ETHIOPIAN HEDGEHOG (7 to 9 in. long). Of Israel's three species of hedgehog, this is the least known. Found in the Negev. Like all hedgehogs, it is not a fast runner. Eats insects, mice, and snakes—even poisonous ones, and some vegetable matter. When frightened, rolls up into a ball of sharp spines. Lives in burrows.

Paraechinus aethiopicus pectoralis

JERBOA (about 4 in. long, tail 7 in.). Two species are found chiefly in the south. Similar to the Kangaroo Rat, it can leap as far as 4 feet, using its long tail for balance and support. Short front legs are only used to hold food. Feeds mainly on seeds. Can live without drinking water.

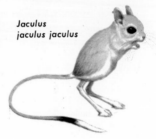

Jaculus jaculus jaculus

ETRUSCAN SHREW (about 1½ in. long) is the smallest known mammal and one of four species of shrews in Israel. Seldom weighs more than 1/10 of an ounce. Hides in piles of straw and in weeds. Despite its small size, it needs a lot of food (insects) and on cold nights often eats more than its own weight.

Suncus etruscus etruscus

BIRDS OF THE HOLY LAND

Nearly 400 species of birds are known in the Holy Land, but of these only about 100 are residents, the others being migrants, summer visitors or winter visitors. Israel is in the middle of one of the great migration routes from eastern Europe and western Asia to Africa and back, and there is an almost constant movement of birds. December and January are the only months in which some migration does not normally take place. The man-made changes which have taken place over the past half-century have, of course, affected bird life, particularly in Israel. Some species have begun to breed in the country for the first time; some have been destroyed, while others, such as some of the former inhabitants of now-vanished swamps, have had to find new homes, often in the sanctuaries and reserves set aside for them. Most of the birds on the following pages have been associated with the Holy Land for thousands of years, and many are mentioned in the Bible. Sizes indicated are from bill tip to tail tip.

PALESTINE BULBUL (6 in.). This resident is one of the few members of its family to live outside the tropics. Always seen in pairs. Young birds eat insects but adults are vegetarian.

HOOPOE (11 in.) arrives in February, leaves in September, but some stay through the winter. Found in north and center. Call is distinctive, low "poo poo." Flight lazy and undulating.

Pycnonotus barbatus xanthopygos

Upupa epops

Podiceps cristatus 1

Halcyon smyrnensis 4

Ciconia ciconia

Pelecanus onocrotalus 2

5

Ardeola ibis 3

6

Hoplopterus spinosus

1 GREAT CRESTED GREBE (19 in.). This large and expert diver is a resident of Holy Land. Black-necked Grebe (38 in.) is a winter visitor.

2 WHITE PELICAN (55 to 70 in.) is passing migrant often seen nesting in Huleh Reserve. Pouch, used in catching fish and straining food, can hold 3 gallons.

3 CATTLE EGRET (20 in.), a resident also known as Buff-backed Heron, is one of 11 herons in Israel. Often stands on the back of an animal, picking off ticks.

4 SMYRNA KINGFISHER (7 in.), a colorful, solitary resident. Lives in a gallery which widens into a chamber where it lays 4 or 5 white, shiny eggs.

5 WHITE STORK (40 in.) is seen in flocks from February until May, soaring or standing still, sometimes with wing outstretched to warm itself in the sun.

6 SPUR-WINGED PLOVER (10 in.) is a resident, seen in fields or near water, in pairs or small flocks. Its call is a noisy "zac-zac-zee."

Merops apiaster

Onychognathus tristramii

Hirundo daurica

Apus apus

Galerida cristata

EUROPEAN BEE-EATER (6 in.). Breeds in the north and center of Israel. Seen from March to October resting on telegraph poles. Catches insects on the wing.

TRISTRAM'S GRACKLE (7 in.). A sweet-singing resident swallow found usually near the Dead Sea. Lays 3 to 5 pale blue eggs in rock cleft nests. Can be tamed.

RED RUMPED SWALLOW (7 in.). A summer breeder seen from March to October. Builds enclosed nest with spout-shape entrance out of tiny, round mud bricks.

SWIFT (6 in.). A spring breeder seen from February to June. Very rapid flight and shrill screech. Large flocks can be seen and heard over large towns.

CRESTED LARK (6 in.), a common resident, seen in open country. Plumper and paler than the Skylark, its song (a liquid "twee-tee-too") is also less musical.

WHITE WAGTAIL (7 in.). A rare resident but a common and popular visitor from October to April. The Black-headed Wagtail breeds in the Jordan Valley.

ARABIAN BABBLER (6 in.). A resident of this south Asian and African family seen mainly around the Dead Sea, whose chattering choruses are reminiscent of human laughter.

Motacilla alba

Turdoides squamiceps

Parus major

Nectarinia oseae

PALESTINE GREAT TIT (4 in.). Northern insect-eating resident, builds mattress-like nest in holes of trees, drainpipes, and walls.

PALESTINE SUNBIRD (2 in.) is the smallest bird in Israel and Jordan. Drinking nectar from flowers, it is often mistaken for a hummingbird.

GREENFINCH (6 in.). This resident is the sweetest songster in the Holy Land. A common seed-eater of gardens and fields. Nests from April to July.

Chloris chloris

Carduelis carduelis

GOLDFINCH (4 in.). A sociable, singing resident seen in gardens, orchards, and fields. Flocks often forage for food on the roadside in fall and winter.

CHAFFINCH (6 in.). A common winter visitor. Flight call is a low "tsip-tsip," song is a cascade of several notes ending in "choo-ee-o."

Fringilla coelebs

GRACEFUL WARBLER (3 in.) is widespread in the Holy Land. Identifiable by circular motion of its long tail and low chirp. Nest is purse-shaped.

DEAD SEA SPARROW (3 in.), a summer breeder, found only in the southern part of Jordan Valley and around the Dead Sea. Builds large nests in tamarisk bushes.

Prinia gracilis

Passer moabiticus

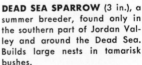

Athene noctua

Clamator glandarius

Streptopellia senegalensis

Pterocles alchata

Coturnix coturnix

Alectoris chukar

1 LITTLE OWL (8 in.). Bobs and bows when frightened. Like the eagle, stork, raven, and pelican, it is a bird which, according to the Bible, Jews are forbidden to eat. Eagle Owl is over 20 in.

2 GREAT SPOTTED CUCKOO (15 in.). A summer breeder in the north and center, it lays its eggs mostly in the nests of the Hooded Crow. A noisy bird, it sometimes sounds like a hen.

3 PIN-TAILED SANDGROUSE is pigeon-like desert bird with feathered feet. Flocks to water morning and evening. Young can run as soon as hatched. Five other species in Israel.

4 PALM DOVE (6 in.). A resident summer breeder related to the common Turtle Dove. Drowsy, persistent "coo-coo" is probably the "voice of the turtle" referred to in Bible as sign of spring.

5 ROCK PARTRIDGE (13 in.), or Chukar, a resident throughout the Holy Land, is a popular game bird. Nests among rocks and lays 6 to 15 pinkish-yellow eggs in April and May.

6 QUAIL (7 in.). A passing migrant, it breeds mostly in rough pastures. Together with manna, quail was eaten in the desert by the Children of Israel during the exodus from Egypt.

1 ROLLER (12 in.). A passing migrant and summer breeder, this jay-like bird is seen in open fields and by the wayside. Feeds on insects, frogs and lizards.

2 BONELLI'S EAGLE (26 to 29 in.). A resident, it swoops on rabbits and birds, hunts falcons. Its relative, the Spotted Eagle, is a passing migrant and a winter visitor.

3 RAVEN (25 in.), the largest of the crow family, can be seen all over the Holy Land. Often seen soaring. Cry is a characteristic, deep, harsh "koarrp."

4 LESSER KESTREL (13 in.). Glides and hovers, plunging steeply to catch mice, beetles, etc. The rare sooty falcon breeds near Dead Sea.

5 EGYPTIAN VULTURE (23 to 26 in.). A summer breeder, nests on cliffs, mostly in caves. One of several species of vulture in Holy Land, it has beautiful flight but is clumsy on the ground.

6 SYRIAN JAY (13 in.). This resident is found mostly in the Carmel Range, near Jerusalem and in the Upper Galilee. Is known for its ability to imitate other birds and even cats.

1 *Coracias garrulus*

Hieraetus fasciatus
2

Falco nauman
4

Neophron percnopterus
5

Corvus corax
3

Garrulus glandarius atricapillus
6

45

INSECTS AND OTHER ARTHROPODS

Experts estimate that there may be some 70,000 species of insects in the Holy Land, of which only some 40,000 have as yet been described. Repeated destruction of towns in the past, present-day afforestation, the introduction of new plants and flowers, the draining of swamps, and irrigation have all served to increase the number and kind of Israel's insects and other arthropods. Among the most common are scorpions, butterflies (over 1,000 species), ants, crickets, praying mantises (more than 15 species), beetles, centipedes, bees.

Danaus chrysippus

Daphnis nerii

SDOM BUTTERFLY (2 in.), seen in lower Jordan Valley and around Ein Gedi. Caterpillars are immune to poison of the Sdom apple.

OLEANDER MOTH (2½ in.). Feeds on poisonous oleander leaves. Its caterpillars have yellow "horn" on the last back segment.

JUDEAN SCORPION (2 to 3 in.). **JERICHO SCORPION** (6 to 7 in.). Both hide by day and move slowly. They are dangerous to small animals and children.

GOLIATH SPIDER (body 1½ in.). Not a true spider, is often mistaken for tarantula. Nocturnal, it hides by day. Not poisonous.

Buthus judaicus

Galeodes orientalis

ALMOND BORER (1¼ in.). Adults feed on stone fruit trees such as almonds, apricots, plums, and peaches.

Capnodis carbonaria

ORIENTAL WASP (¾ in. wing). Sting can be fatal to man. Nests made of papier-maché of tree bark, soil, and saliva. Raids bee-hives.

Vespa orientalis

GIANT GRASSHOPPER (5 to 7 in.). Holy Land's largest insect. Wingless carnivore, it feeds on insects and small animals.

Saga ephippigera

Blepharopsis mendica nuda

Anacridium aegyptium

PRAYING MANTIS (2½ in.), or King Solomon's Camel. Female devours male's head at mating. Moves so slowly victim is caught unawares.

JUDEAN CENTIPEDE (4 in.) has at least 40 legs. First pair of legs give painful sting. Lives under stones and bark in the north.

DESERT LOCUST (2½ in.) was one of the Ten Plagues of Egypt during exodus. Swarms from Sudan about once every 30 years.

SCARAB BEETLE (1 in.). Sacred to ancient Egyptians. Seen on coastal sand dunes, rolling dung balls, some used as egg depositories.

Scolopendra cingulata

Scarabaeus sacer

Marble griffin dated to 3rd century found near Erez in southern Israel

ARCHEOLOGY
IN THE HOLY LAND

Since the fourth millenium B.C., the Holy Land has been the crossroads of different cultures, and has served as a land bridge between the continents of Europe, Africa, and Asia. Its place in archeology is unique. The first modern excavation of a Palestinian site was made in 1850 by a French explorer, but the earliest scientific archeological work is dated from 1865, when the Palestine Exploration Fund was established and excavations started in Jerusalem.

In 1870, the American Palestine Exploration Society began its work. The best known of the early Palestine archeologists was Flinders Petrie, who first introduced a systematic recording of finds and used pottery for dating.

Excavations in Israel take place in "seasons"—sometimes four seasons to a summer. At the end of each season, the finds are removed for study, research, and eventual display.

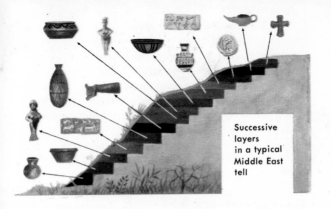

Successive layers in a typical Middle East tell

A TELL (above) is a flat-topped artificial mound, common in the Middle East. It is made up of a series of destroyed villages and cities, with the oldest layer of human occupation at the bottom. With each new settlement, the area for building became smaller, giving the tell its peculiar shape. The number of layers can vary from one, as in the Chalcolithic settlement of Beersheba, to 23, spanning centuries from the Early Bronze age to Hellenistic times, as in Hazor. A tell must be excavated by hand to prevent destruction of its contents.

Important museums in Israel are: In Jerusalem, the Israel Museum and the Shrine of The Book next to the Hebrew University; The Museum of Religious Antiquities at the Chief Rabbinate; the Herbert E. Clark collection at the YMCA; the Museum of the Biblical Pontifical Institute, and the Palestine Museum, a gift of John D. Rockefeller, Jr. In Tel Aviv, the "Ha'aretz" complex of museums and the Tel Aviv-Jaffa Antiquities Museum in Jaffa. In Haifa, the Municipal Museum of Ancient Art, the Ethnological Museum, and the "Dagon" Archeological Collection.

THE DEAD SEA SCROLLS are among the greatest of all modern archeological finds. In spring 1947, a Bedouin shepherd discovered on the cliffs over Khirbet Qumran, at the northwest end of the Dead Sea, a cave which contained eight earthenware jars. Inside, he found bundles of parchment wrapped in linen, which turned out to be ancient Hebrew manuscripts, dating as far back as the first century B.C.

The discovery remained unnoticed for many months, and the manuscripts passed from hand to hand. Their significance gradually became known in the following years. International teams of scholars set out to study them, and expeditions were sent to look for more. The Dead Sea Scrolls were found to contain complete manuscripts of the Book of Isaiah, a commentary on the Biblical Book of Habbakuk (Jewish prophet of the 7th century B.C.), an apocalyptic poem telling of the struggle between the Sons of Light and the Sons of Darkness, and psalms. Since then, fragments of every book of the Hebrew Bible except Esther have been identified. Of the hundreds of scrolls that have been found near the Dead Sea, many are dispersed in institutions throughout the world.

Unrolling a Dead Sea scroll

In 1951, Bedouin tribesmen discovered more scrolls on the steep hills near the Wadi Murabaat, some 10 miles south of Qumran. These scrolls, in Hebrew, Greek, and Aramaic (the language used by Jesus) were more recent—first century B.C. and first and second century A.D.—and were probably hidden during the second Jewish uprising. Among them were four letters by Bar Kochba, a Jewish leader during the revolt against the Romans (A.D. 135).

There was, among the scrolls, a "Manual of Discipline" which sets down rules and regulations for a monastic Jewish sect, probably the Essenes, to which John the Baptist may have belonged. Not much is known about the Essenes. It is believed that, in protest against licentiousness, they formed an austere sect, were persecuted, and took refuge near the Dead Sea. They are mentioned in Pliny's *Natural History,* and documents found in a Cairo synagogue mention their exodus to Damascus.

The State of Israel has acquired several scrolls, which are on permanent exhibit in the Shrine of the Book of the Israel National Museum in Jerusalem. Other scrolls are in the Palestine Archeological Museum in Jerusalem.

The Shrine of the Book

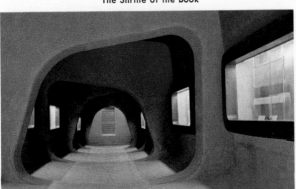

THE PAST

PRE-HISTORY The land of the Bible has long been the focus of intense archeological interest. Perhaps as far back as a million years ago in the Lower Paleolithic Age, when elephants and hippopotami roamed the jungles which then covered the land, primitive man in the Jordan Valley already made tools from pebbles. About 100,000 years ago, Neanderthal Man appeared in the caves of the Galilee, the Carmel Mountains, and the Judean Desert. Later he became extinct.

At about 30,000 B.C. he was followed by Homo sapiens. From 15,000 B.C. the climate became what it is now—long hot summers and short rainy winters—and man left his caves for the first time to live outdoors. By 8,000 B.C. the Natufian Culture (named for Wadi Natufa in the hills of Judea), had produced houses and the beginnings of art and of agriculture. With the Neolithic Era (the new Stone Age) came intensive agriculture and the domestication of animals. Perhaps the world's oldest known town, Jericho, was built then. During this era, (7500-4000 B.C.), the Yarmuk Culture flourished. Named for the excavation site near the River Yarmuk in the northern part of the Jordan Valley, where beautiful fertility figures have been found, it has to its credit one of mankind's great discoveries—the making of pottery.

CHALCOLITHIC copper objects found in a cave of the Judean desert near the Dead Sea

BEIT YERACH means House of the Moon in Hebrew. Lake Tiberias is in background

Excavations of the Chalcolithic period——the Copper-Stone Age of the 4th millenium B.C.——have brought to light a civilization with a highly developed copper industry. At Nahal Mishmar near the Dead Sea, some 400 copper and ivory tools, mace-heads, staves, and standards were found wrapped in a mat. These people first built underground houses, then huts with storage pits, and finally timber-roofed cottages. During the second millenium B.C. the empires of the Middle East in the valleys of the Nile and the Euphrates started taking shape.

A massive early Bronze Age city (early 4th millenium) was found in Beit Yerach, a few miles south of Tiberias. It was ringed by a 25-foot wall (later rebuilt by Solomon) and boasted giant grain silos. Like most of the Holy Land's historic sites, this settlement was covered over by a series of subsequent communities. Beit Yerach was destroyed, probably in the 24th century B.C., and built up again later. It has remnants of a 4th century A.D. synagogue, a 5th century A.D. Roman bathhouse, and a 6th century A.D. Byzantine church.

EARLY ART from Holy Land: Copper standard, dated to end of 4th millenium B.C., and Canaanite figurines

With the Bronze Age, an urban civilization started to develop—the civilization of the Canaanites, who lived in independent, fortified city-states, each under its own king, each worshipping its own Gods. Jericho and Hazor, mentioned in the Book of Joshua, are characteristic of this era. From the beginning of their history, these city-states were prey to the great empires of Mesopotamia and Egypt, and all were harried by roving bands of invaders.

HAZOR 4th millenium Canaanite city destroyed by Joshua at the end of the 13th century B.C.

TEL QUASILE was established in the 12th century B.C. Here, a furnace for melting bronze

BIBLICAL TIMES Today, the background of even the earliest stories of the Bible has been largely proven historically correct. During the 2nd millenium B.C., Abraham of Ur led his clan from Mesopotamia into Canaan, where they settled. Clay tablets, excavated at Mari on the Euphrates, provide evidence of similar tribal movements during this period. The Patriarchs—Abraham, his son Isaac, and his grandson Jacob, whose second name was Israel—are buried in a cave in Hebron. About the 14th century B.C., Jacob's son, Joseph, was sold into slavery by his brothers and taken to Egypt where, later, driven by drought, they joined him. The descendants of Jacob's twelve sons—Reuben, Simeon, Judah, Dan, Naphtali, Gad, Asher, Levi, Issachar, Zebulun, Benjamin, and Joseph—formed the twelve tribes of Israel. Joseph's own tribe was divided between his two sons, Ephraim and Menasseh. Each of the tribes was allotted part of the Promised Land upon their return from Egypt, except for the priestly house of Levi, to which no specific territory was given.

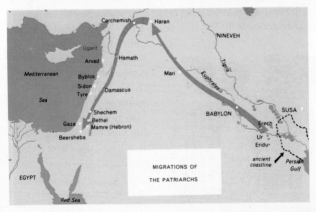

MIGRATIONS OF THE PATRIARCHS

About 1375 B.C., Moses led the Children of Israel out of Egypt and across the Wilderness of Sinai up to the borders of the land which God had promised Abraham. Moses died, but the Israelites crossed the Jordan, near Jericho, under the command of Joshua, who conquered western Canaan, marking the end of a little-known ancient Canaanite civilization. By about 1200 B.C. the Israelite infiltration of Canaan was deep but control was still weak. The land was under constant attack by the surviving Canaanites, the neighboring peoples, and later by the sea-going Philistines from Gaza, Ashkelon, Ashdod, Ekron, and Gath along the Mediterranean coast. In their attempts to hold their territory, the Israelites united over a period of two hundred years under a succession of secular "spontaneous" leaders, known as the "Judges," of whom the most popular was Samson. The Philistines, however, eventually dominated large parts of the country, which later became known as Palestine—the Land of the Philistines.

The exploits of Samson, who, blinded, pulled down the Philistine temple of Dagon, and the battle of young David against Goliath, are part of the struggle of the

Hebrews against the Philistines, who eventually captured the Sacred Ark of the Covenant, a transportable temple. The last and greatest judge was the prophet Samuel, who anointed the first king, Saul.

Asiatic people, from an ancient Egyptian wall painting

DAVID AND SOLOMON

The threat of subjugation by the Philistines forced the Israelite tribes to form a kingdom, first under Saul (1025-1006 B.C.) and then under David (1004-965 B.C.). David made Jerusalem the religious and administrative center of the new kingdom. He united the northern and southern tribes, conquered Damascus and parts of Lebanon, wiped out remaining Canaanite enclaves, and defeated the Philistines. He extended Israelite influence to the Euphrates and along the Mediterranean coast to Tyre and Sidon. When King David died, he bequeathed his kingdom to Solomon, his son (965-922 B.C.), establishing a dynasty which reigned in Jerusalem for 400 years.

Solomon was not a conquering warrior, but he consolidated his father's conquests. He set up a chain of fortified cities to protect his kingdom and concentrated on commerce. He turned Israel into a center of trade, developed a copper mining and smelting industry in the Negev and built a port for trade with Africa. He married the daughter of an Egyptian Pharaoh, and played host to the colorful Queen of Sheba. Solomon undertook vast construction programs, and hired Phoenician craftsmen to build his magnificent Temple in Jerusalem.

ARMAGEDDON is corruption of Har Megiddo, Hebrew for the Hill of Megiddo. In *Revelation*, Megiddo is the site of the battle to be fought at the end of time.

Above is a reconstruction of the Biblical city. Excavations have uncovered 20 layers, the earliest of the Chalcolithic Period, the last of the 4th century B.C.

EXILE TO BABYLON At Solomon's death in 922 B.C. the monarchy split into the northern kingdom of Israel and the southern kingdom of Judah, of which Jerusalem remained the capital. These kingdoms were relentlessly harassed by the rival empires of Egypt, Syria, and Assyria and by internal revolts and assassinations. As a succession of fiery public preachers—the Prophets Elijah, Elisha, Hosea, Amos, and Isaiah—grimly predicted, the weakened kingdom of Israel fell to Assyria while the kingdom of Judah dwindled into a vassal state of the Assyrian Empire. Its end came after Babylon conquered the remnants of the Assyrian Empire (587 B.C.).

AT MEGIDDO, ancient water tunnel to well outside city walls

THE SECOND TEMPLE In 586 B.C. Jerusalem was razed by the Babylonian army. The Temple was destroyed and most of the population exiled to Babylon— until 538 B.C. when Babylon, in its turn, fell to Cyrus of Persia who permitted the Jews to return home. The grandchildren of those who had been taken to Babylon built a second Temple, completed in 515 B.C.

For the next 200 years, the Jews were relatively autonomous although still part of the Persian Empire. In 333 B.C. the armies of Alexander the Great swept through the Middle East and conquered Judea. After Alexander's death, control of Judea passed first into the hands of the Ptolemies of Egypt; then, in 198 B.C., to the Greek-influenced Seleucid Kingdom of Syria.

About 168 B.C., the Syrian king, Antiochus IV Epiphanes, plundered the Temple and consecrated it to the god Zeus. Led by a priestly family—the Hasmoneans —the Jews rebelled in 168 B.C. against increasing Syrian persecution. With Judas Maccabee at their head, they drove the Syrians out of Jerusalem and in 142 B.C. established an independent Hasmonean kingdom which ruled Judea until 63 B.C.

ANTIOCHUS IV EPIPHANES, wearing the Greek diadem

HASMONEAN period drawing of warship pursuing two merchant ships

ROMAN DOMINION Then came the Romans. In 40 B.C., Herod the Great, supported by Rome, was declared "King of Judea." He constructed the port of Caesarea and the fortress of Masada and rebuilt the Temple, adding to its splendor. One wall erected by Herod still stands today in the Old City of Jerusalem—the western wall, better known as the Wailing Wall, to which Jews for centuries came to mourn the destruction of the Temple. Not long before Herod's death, Jesus was born in Bethlehem. In A.D. 6 the Romans annexed Judea, which became a Roman subprovince of Syria. In A.D. 29, under the Roman Procurator (or Imperial Governor) Pontius Pilate, Jesus was crucified in Jerusalem.

In A.D. 66 the Jews again revolted. Roman legions poured into the land and in A.D. 70 the Tenth Legion broke the Jewish rebellion, overpowered Jerusalem, burned the Temple to the ground, and sold thousands of Jews into slavery. One pocket of insurrection still remained. In that desert fort, Masada, which Herod had built not far from the Dead Sea, a group of Jews fought on for three more years. In A.D. 132, another desperate Jewish uprising broke out under Bar Kochba, who was crushed by Emperor Hadrian's legions in A.D. 135.

Scale model of the Temple in Jerusalem

MASADA (a Hellenized form of the Hebrew Metzuda, meaning stronghold) was built by Herod on a huge flat-topped rock jutting out from the Wilderness of Judah, some 1,500 feet above the level of the Dead Sea. There were storehouses, a palace, and cisterns first used by Herod in his battle against the Hasmoneans. In A.D. 73, it fell after a siege by the Roman Tenth Legion; all but five of a thousand of its Jewish defenders were dead. Masada is still being excavated.

JUDEA CAPTA coin commemorating Roman victory in Palestine

PONTIUS PILATE'S name on stone slab found in Caesarea

BYZANTINE RULE   With the fall of the Temple, which had been the focal point of Jewish life in Palestine, Mesopotamia became the new center for Judaism. During the first century, the Christian religion started spreading in the eastern Mediterranean, mainly through Saul of Tarsus—St. Paul. At the beginning of the 4th century Emperor Constantine made Christianity the official religion of the Roman Empire. In A.D. 324, the empire split into two—a western part, ruled from Rome, and an eastern part, ruled from Byzantium (Constantinople). Constantine was enthroned emperor of the Byzantine part. Constantine lavished time and treasure on the land that had cradled his faith. He and his mother, Helena, built scores of churches, of which the most famous is the Church of the Holy Sepulchre in the Old City of Jerusalem. Pilgrims flooded the country, and hundreds of monasteries sprang up. Palestine prospered, although the growth of Byzantine Orthodoxy resulted in persecution of the Jews and of those Christian groups that did not accept the official dogma.

ST. HELENA, mother of Constantine, is said to have discovered Golgotha and the "true cross."

BYZANTINE MOSAIC in Tabgha, one of many in Holy Land

MOSLEM DOMINION The first weakening of Byzantine rule came in A.D. 614 when the Persians captured Jerusalem and held it for 13 years. Byzantine rule finally ended in A.D. 640 when Caesarea, its last stronghold in Palestine, fell to the invading Arabs.

The Moslems constructed a mosque, the Dome of the Rock, in A.D. 691, over the spot where the Temple had once stood and from which Mohammed is believed to have ascended to heaven. Jerusalem became a city holy to Islam. At first, Moslem rule from Damascus was tolerant. But with the transfer of the Moslem political capital to Baghdad in A.D. 762, the attitude of the Caliphate became increasingly hostile, both to Jews and to Christians. When power passed to an Egyptian dynasty, the Fatimids, who founded Cairo in A.D. 973, the situation worsened. Palestine had been under Moslem rule for nearly four centuries, when the order (only partially executed) given in A.D. 1009 by Caliph Hakim to destroy the Holy Sepulchre ignited the Christian Holy Wars. The first Crusade was launched in A.D. 1096.

RAMLA, the only town built by the Moslems in Palestine, was founded in A.D. 716 by Caliph Suleiman. The White Tower, rising 90 feet above ruins of a mosque, was built in the 13th or 14th century. The town was built at the junction of two important caravan routes, south-north from Egypt to Syria, and west-east from the Mediterranean inland. Today, it lies along the main Tel Aviv-Jerusalem highway, the busiest in Israel.

CRUSADER castle in Jordan, and scene from stained glass window

THE CRUSADES Throughout the Holy Land, the remnants of castles, churches, manor houses, and hospices built by the Crusaders can still be seen. Inspired by the preaching of Peter the Hermit and organized by Pope Urban II, the First Crusade (1096-1099) under Godfrey de Bouillon took three years to reach Palestine from France. Twelve thousand Crusaders—nobles and knights, serfs and freemen—captured Jerusalem, and established the Latin Kingdom of Jerusalem, formed on the feudal pattern of medieval Europe, and depending upon it.

The Latin Kingdom, known as Outremer (the land beyond the sea), consisted of the Kingdom of Jerusalem, the counties of Edessa and Tripoli, and the principality of Antioch. Although it lasted less than a hundred years, many churches were built during that time. The Church of the Holy Sepulchre was restored and the Moslem Dome of the Rock in Jerusalem was converted for Christian use. The Moslems, united under the Saracen warrior Saladin, eventually defeated the Crusaders on the plain of the Horns of Hattin, between Tiberias and Nazareth, and retook Jerusalem in A.D. 1187.

16TH CENTURY map of the Holy Land

The Third Crusade (1189-1192) was headed at first by Frederick Barbarossa of the Holy Roman Empire. He drowned in a river before he reached the Holy Land, and many of his well-equipped troops turned back. Richard the Lion-Hearted of England and Philip Augustus of France went on. They quarreled constantly, and Philip returned home. Saladin came out from Jaffa to halt the Crusader armies but Richard, outnumbered 30 to one, fought him to a standstill, although he could not take Jerusalem. The resultant truce, signed in 1192, stipulated that the Christians would hold a narrow strip of the seacoast between Tyre and Jaffa, but that Jerusalem would remain Moslem.

The subsequent Crusades (from 1202 to 1291) to regain Jerusalem were led by the great Christian military orders such as the Templars and the Teutonic Knights, and by such famous historical personalities as Pope Innocent IV, St. Louis (Louis IX of France), and the prince who was to become Edward I of England. However, all of these Crusades failed on the whole.

ST. ANNE, former Crusader church, near Beit-Guvrin

RUINS of Belvoir, a Crusader castle in Israel

Jerusalem changed hands several times, and was finally seized in A.D. 1258 by Saladin's successors, the Egyptian Mamelukes. These were mercenaries, mostly of Georgian and Circassian origin, who reestablished Moslem rule over Palestine, controlling it from Safad and Gaza. The Mamelukes lasted from 1250 to 1516 when they were defeated by the Turkish Sultan, Selim I, who captured Jerusalem. For the next 400 years, Palestine was a Turkish province, governed from Constantinople, the seat of the sultanate which was to provide the country with the most ruinous rule it had ever known.

Turkish aqueduct in Naharia, north of Haifa

THE CRUSADES

First Crusade (1096-1099) led by Godfrey of Bouillon, Raymond of Toulouse, Robert of Flanders, and Robert of Normandy—resulted in the conquest of Jerusalem and creation of the Latin Kingdom.

Second Crusade (1147-1148) led by Conrad III of Germany and Louis VII of France—was organized in response to the fall of the principality of Edessa and ended in failure.

Third Crusade (1189-1192) led by Richard I (the Lion-Hearted) of England, Philip II of France, Frederick I (Barbarossa) of Germany—resulted in a truce with Saladin and establishment of a second Latin Kingdom.

Fourth Crusade (1201-1204) known as the "Constantinople Crusade" —inspired by Pope Innocent III and led by Philip of Swabia, Baldwin of Flanders, and Theobald III of Champagne. Aimed at the conquest of Egypt, it ended with the Crusader conquest of Christian Constantinople in 1204.

Children's Crusade (1212) 20,000 children led from Germany by a child from Cologne, and from France by a young shepherd, got no farther than Marseilles and Genoa. Its child-troops either died en route or were kidnapped and sold into slavery.

Fifth Crusade (1217-1221) led by Andrew of Hungary and Leopold VI of Austria fought in Palestine and failed in its attempted conquest of Egypt.

Sixth Crusade (1228-1229) led by Frederick II, Emperor of Germany, achieved (by negotiation, not by fighting) the recovery of Jerusalem, in Moslem hands since 1187, as well as Nazareth and Bethlehem. The Kingdom of Jerusalem now comprised western Galilee, the Bay of Haifa, the Sharon Plain, and the Jerusalem Corridor. In 1266, Jerusalem was lost to Baibars, the future Mameluke Sultan of Egypt.

Seventh Crusade (1248) led by St. Louis of France against Egypt, was routed. In 1250, St. Louis reached Acre where he remained for four years, and fortified Haifa, Caesarea, Jaffa, etc.

In 1263, Baibars attacked and destroyed most of the Crusader strongholds in the Holy Land.

Eighth Crusade (1270) St. Louis commanded another Crusade (with the future Edward I of England). He hoped to conquer Tunis, but died at Carthage. In 1271, Prince Edward, the last of the Crusaders, led his own, unsuccessful Crusade to Acre. In 1291, Acre fell to Baibars' grandson and the kingdom of Jerusalem came to an end.

SULEIMAN TO NAPOLEON BONAPARTE In 1538
Suleiman I (Selim's son), rebuilt the walls which still enclose Jerusalem today, repaired its water supply, and organized the land tenure system. But within a century Turkish interest in the development of Palestine declined and Palestine's trade, industry, agriculture, and population all came to a virtual standstill.

Turkish overlords, or Pashas, became more or less independent of the weak central Government. The most famous of these was Ahmed el Jazzar (1775-1804), "The Butcher," who fortified Acre and defended it, with British help, against Bonaparte in 1799. After two months of fighting, Bonaparte, who had marched into the Holy Land after his conquest of Egypt, withdrew.

In 1831, Turkish Palestine and Syria were invaded by the Egyptians, who rebelled against Turkish rule. The Egyptians took over the rule in both countries for nine years, until they were driven out in 1840 by the European allies of the Turkish Sultan.

13th or 14th century Mosque lamp, and Arab jewelry

Zionist "Shomrim," Jewish armed watchmen, in 1907

THE RISE OF MODERN ISRAEL By the end of the 19th century, a new factor appeared: the Zionist movement, named for Zion, once the site of the Temple, and a symbol of Judaism.

The Jewish link with Palestine had remained unbroken. Here and there, in the old Jewish quarters of Jerusalem, Safad, Tiberias, and Hebron, a few thousand impoverished artisans and scholars devoted their lives to religious studies. But in the 1880's after increasing persecution of the Jews in Russia, the feeling grew among the Jews of Europe that a concrete solution must be found if the Jewish people were to survive. The Zionist movement formally came into being in Switzerland in 1897. It drafted plans for a mass return of the Jews to Palestine and for the creation of a Jewish Home. The founder of the World Zionist Organization, Dr. Theodor Herzl, a Viennese journalist, had visited Palestine in 1896, and traveled throughout Europe to enlist support for his plan. Deganiah, "The Cornflower," founded in 1909, was the first Jewish collective settlement (kibbutz).

THE BRITISH MANDATE In 1910 the first houses of an all-Jewish city, Tel Aviv, rose on the sand dunes north of Jaffa. By 1914, there were 47 Jewish agricultural settlements in Turkish Palestine, most of them on land owned by the Jewish National Fund, purchased with contributions from Jews the world over. Turkey entered World War I on the side of Germany. In 1917 a Jewish military formation—the Jewish Legion (as part of the conquering British Army)—landed in Palestine. In November, 1917, the British published the Balfour Declaration, which announced that the Government viewed with favor the establishment in Palestine of a National Home for the Jewish people. In December, 1917, Britain's Field Marshal Allenby received the surrender of Jerusalem from the Turks.

The League of Nations allotted the Mandate over Palestine to Great Britain in 1920. The first British High Commissioner, a Jew, was appointed in 1920. Arab leaders opposed the development of the Jewish State, but the Jews formed their own defense organization and developed an independent, economic, and cultural life. By the beginning of World War II, the Jews in Israel numbered just under half a million. Jewish immigration had to be restricted, but immigration continued illegally through the 1940's.

MEMORIAL from the 1948 Israel War of Independence was made of the rusty carcasses of armored trucks destroyed during fighting on the road from the coast to Jerusalem.

THE PROCLAMATION OF THE STATE   In 1947, the last of many British and international commissions of inquiry recommended the partitioning of Palestine into a Jewish and an Arab State, a proposal which was accepted by the United Nations. On May 15, 1948, the British withdrew, and the state of Israel was proclaimed. David Ben Gurion was the first Prime Minister. The War of Independence, punctuated by truces, lasted until the middle of 1949, when armistices were signed, and Israel's frontiers delineated. But peace was not declared. About a third of the Arab population elected to stay in Israel, the rest fled to the surrounding Arab countries (most of them to Jordan). Border incidents multiplied. In October, 1956, the Israeli Army advanced towards the Suez Canal. With their withdrawal in March, 1957, a United Nations Emergency Force took over the patroling of the Israel-Egypt border. In June, 1967, following the withdrawal of UNEF, a brief war broke out between Israel and the surrounding Arab countries, resulting in the military defeat of the latter.

Today Israel is a parliamentary republic whose President is elected for five years. Legislative power is vested in the Knesset, a chamber of 120 members elected by universal suffrage. The Cabinet, headed by the Prime Minister, is responsible to the Knesset.

KNESSET, or assembly, building is in Jerusalem. Assembly is named after *Haknesset Hagdola*, 120-man lawgiving body of Jews during the Persian rule of Israel which started in 550 B.C.

MODERN ISRAEL

THE PEOPLE One of the first laws passed by the Knesset when the State of Israel was proclaimed gave all Jews the right to settle in Israel. Within three years the Jewish population of 655,000 was doubled. In the first ten years of Israel's existence, a million Jews immigrated into it from all over the world, most of them with no financial means. World Jewry raised the enormous funds required to finance the immigration and settle the newcomers on the land. Airlifts were organized to transport them; "Operation Magic Carpet" flew in all the 50,000 Jews of Yemen, in southern Arabia, and "Operation Ali Baba" brought in the Jews of Iraq. At first, the newcomers lived in makeshift camps. Later, they were given permanent homes. Some went to the big cities, but most were settled in new towns in the Galilee and the Negev, where they could work either in agriculture or light industry. One of the most advanced of these areas is Lachish, the site of a former Canaanite city destroyed by Joshua in the 13th century B.C. Special courses, *ulpanim,* were set up to teach Hebrew to tens of thousands of adults.

Israeli Independence Day

Druse festivities and dances

THE HEBREW LANGUAGE

After the 6th century B.C., Hebrew (a language closely related to Canaanite and Phoenician) ceased to be the major language of the Jews, and Aramaic, an ancient Semitic language, took its place. Hebrew was reserved for prayer and study, and only some 7,000 words were in use. In 1881, a Russian Jewish journalist, Eliezer Ben Yehuda, settled in Palestine, and compiled a dictionary which listed thousands of old words and hundreds of new ones, which he formed mainly from ancient Hebrew roots. In 1920, Hebrew, with Arabic and English, became one of the country's three official languages. Hebrew and Arabic are the official languages of Israel today, and English is taught in school. The development of Hebrew, which now has over 50,000 words, is entrusted to the Hebrew Language Academy.

ALPHABET	NAME	TRANS-LITERATION	NUMBER
א	ALEF	–	1
ב	BET	B or V	2
ג	GIMEL	G	3
ד	DALET	D	4
ה	HAY	H	5
ו	VAV	V	6
ז	ZAYIN	Z	7
ח	KHET	Kh	8
ט	TET	T	9
י	YOD	I or Y	10
ך כ	KAF	Kh	20
ל	LAMED	L	30
ם מ	MEM	M	40
ן נ	NUN	N	50
ס	SAMEKH	S	60
ע	AYIN	–	70
ף פ	PAY	P or F	80
ץ צ	TSADE	Ts	90
ק	KUF	Q or K	100
ר	RESH	R	200
ש	SHIN	Sh or S	300
ת	TAV	T or Th	400

HEBREW ALPHABET Language is written from right to left. Letters are shown with their name, spelled in English and transliterated. Letters may also represent numbers. Vowels are either omitted, or represented by special signs.

1. Immigrant from Cochin India

2. Yemenite Jew

3. Copt

4. Jewish woman from Iraq

5. Yemenite immigrants

6. Israeli women in the army

7. Moroccan immigrant

8. Kibbutznik in Ein Gedi

9. Kibbutz girl on annual march

10. Old Bedouin woman

11. Bedouin shepherdess spins wool.

12. Arab shepherd

SIX-POINTED STAR OF DAVID has been a symbol of Judaism since the Middle Ages. Above, in Capernaum

MENORAH is the lamp which lit the altar of the Temple. It is represented in the design of the Israel State seal.

JUDAISM is the world's oldest monotheistic faith. It is a faith without saints, without a hierarchy, and without missionaries. It is not proselytizing: it does not try to make converts. Judaism today has no central place of worship although in ancient times this was the function of the Temple. The synagogue is a house of both prayer and of study; rabbis are teachers and leaders of the congregation but not regarded as more holy than their flock.

Nine-tenths of Israel's two and a half million people are Jewish. For the most part, Israel's Jews are neither more nor less religious than Jews elsewhere, but the traditions of Judaism, particularly of its holy days and festivals, are imprinted on the everyday life of the country. Rabbinical courts have kept, since the time of the Turks, sole jurisdiction in Jewish marriage and divorce and in certain other matters. Traditionally, a Jew is a person whose mother was a Jew.

CHIEF RABBINATE is in Jerusalem. Rabbinical courts have jurisdiction in certain personal matters.

CHAGALL'S stained glass windows in Hadassah Hospital symbolize the Tribes of Israel. Here, Naphtali

For all Jews, the Sabbath starts on Friday evening, ends on Saturday at sundown, and is the official day of rest. There is almost no public transportation on the Sabbath; shops, government offices, public institutions, and theatres are closed. Because many of Israel's Jews are orthodox, the state educational system encompasses both secular and religious schools where children are taught the history, geography, and language of their land, as well as other subjects.

Jewish ritual dietary laws (kashrut) are enforced in the army, in all hospitals, on Israeli ships and aircraft, and in most large hotels. Two distinctive features of Israel's spiritual landscape are the religious collective settlements which farm their land according to Jewish laws (among them the sabbatical year, during which fields are allowed to rest) and the specifically religious political parties represented in the Knesset. Israel has over 4,000 synagogues.

Bukharan Jews celebrate Passover.

Scribe copies Torah.

THE TORAH (or Law) is summarized in the Five Books of Moses (Genesis, Exodus, Leviticus, Numbers, Deuteronomy) and still serves as the basis of Jewish religious law. Although hundreds of rules and regulations (dealing with the organization of a Jewish society, with economics, agriculture, etc., as well as with basic ethics) are contained in the Torah, the basic credo of Judaism is set down in the Book of Deuteronomy, where it is written: "Hear O Israel, the Lord our God, the Lord is One." The Ten Commandments are followed by the laws that help carry them out.

Rabbis of antiquity knew the Torah by heart and believed that all aspects of human behavior could be guided by its interpretation. As time passed, the sages had to memorize not only the Torah but a massive body of commentaries and rulings. With the dispersion of the Jews (Diaspora) these were written down and are known as the Talmud.

Sabbath in Hebrew means rest. Jews are enjoined to keep the seventh day completely free of work, given to study and contemplation. Special prayers and chants, as well as special foods, are part of the celebration.

Eating matzot, unleavened bread   Purim spring carnival

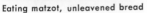

CUSTOMS AND TRADITIONS   The most widely practiced of the Jewish customs are those which mark the stages of man's life. The *Brith Milah,* circumcision of Jewish boys on the eighth day after birth, symbolizes the everlasting covenant between God and the Jews. The *Bar-Mitzvah,* a boy's 13th birthday, makes him a full member of his community. For the first time, he is permitted to wear *tefillin* at his morning prayers. These are two leather boxes containing portions of the Torah, which are worn on the left arm and forehead. Observant Jews over 13 wear a *tallith,* or fringed prayer shawl, in synagogue. They wear a skullcap or a hat at all times, from childhood on, to remind them that God is above them. Religious women cover their hair.

Weddings take place under a canopy. The marriage contract is read. The ring must be plain and without stones. At the end of the ceremony, the groom breaks a glass in memory of the destruction of the Temple.

Jewish women are entrusted with the task of maintaining the customs pertaining to the household—chiefly, upholding the dietary rules of *kashrut;* for instance, meat and dairy dishes must be kept separate.

79

ARABS In addition to two-and-a-quarter million Jews living in some 70 cities and towns and 750 villages, there are some 250,000 Arabs in Israel, who live in eight towns and 100 villages, mainly in Galilee, and cultivate over 300,000 acres.

Most of the Arabs are Moslem. Islam, meaning submission (to God's will) is the youngest of the three great monotheistic religions, and has 300 million faithful. The first year of the Moslem calendar is A.D. 622, the year of *Hegira*, the flight of Mohammed from Mecca after he denounced Arab idolatry. Moslems accept both the Old and the New Testaments, revere Biblical prophets and Jesus. But Mohammed is first among the prophets, and his words constitute the Koran.

In Israel, Arabic is an official language, appearing together with Hebrew on coins, stamps, bank notes, and in official publications. The language of instruction in Arab schools in Israel is Arabic, with Hebrew being taught as a second language. Moslem religious courts have jurisdiction in matters of personal status for Moslems (marriage, divorce, etc.), and Israel has some 120 mosques, notably, the Great Mosque of El-Jazzar.

El-Jazzar Mosque in Acre

Leading Minorities in Israel	
Moslem	202,000
Druse	28,000
Greek Catholic	22,000
Greek Orthodox	16,500
Roman Catholic	10,000
Maronite	2,800
Protestant	2,000
Monophysite	1,500
(Armenian, Gregorian, Coptic)	
Bahai	150

MINORITIES Among the largest Arab minorities in the Holy Land are the Druse, a Moslem community which broke away from Islam in the 11th century. They believe in the divinity of Khalif Hakim (996-1020) and are named after his apostle, Ismail Darazi, who left Egypt to spread his secret religion through Syria. Most of the Druse are in Syria and Lebanon.

The Circassians are a Moslem group, whose ancestors came from the Russian Caucasus in the 19th century. There are some 10,000 in Jordan, and 2,000 in Israel.

The Bahai sect, established by Ali Nuri Baha Allah, exiled to Acre by the Sultan in 1868, emphasize such principles as charity, humility, and love of one's neighbor. Bahaism has more than a million followers in the U.S., Canada, Japan, and India, but only a few hundred in the Holy Land. The Bahai temple on Mount Carmel, burial place of Baha Allah, is the center of Bahaism.

The Karaites accept only the literal law of the Bible. Most of them live near Ramla. The Samaritans are an ancient sect who recognize only the first five books of the Old Testament and Joshua. Some live in Israel, mostly near Tel Aviv; the others are all in Jordan.

Druse leaders

Bahai temple in Haifa

Pope Paul VI in Hall of Last Supper

Benedictine monk on Mount Zion

CHRISTIANS   The Christian community in Jordan and Israel exceeds 200,000 with about 55,000 of them living in Israel. Most of the Christians are Arabs whose ancestors were converted during the Crusades. The rest are chiefly of European origin, members of religious orders in charge of holy sites, hospices, and schools. There are also a number of interesting but little known ancient Christian minorities. The main Christian denominations are the Catholic, Orthodox, Monophysite, and the Protestant.

Among the Catholics, the majority are Greek Catholic who are subject to the authority of the Patriarch of Antioch and of all the Orient, who resides either in Damascus or in Cairo. Services are conducted chiefly in Arabic. The Maronites, or Syrian Catholics (from Jean Maron, founder of the church in the 7th century), have been united with Rome since the Crusades. Their Patriarch in Lebanon receives Papal confirmation. Roman Catholic monks and nuns are headed by the Latin Patriarch in the Old City of Jerusalem. Franciscans have custody of most of the Christian holy sites.

Coptic service in Jerusalem   Russian Orthodox service

The Eastern Orthodox Church, independent of Rome, has four patriarchates: Constantinople, Jerusalem, Antioch, and Alexandria. There are several Greek and Russian Orthodox churches or monasteries on some of the most important holy sites.

The Monophysites differ from Catholic and Orthodox churches in that they recognize only one nature of Jesus, while the Ecumenical Council of Chalcedonia (451) had defined two closely linked but distinct natures, one human, one divine. The Monophysites eventually split into three churches, which have a few thousand members in the Holy Land: The Armenian Church, whose Patriarch or *Catholicos* resides in Turkey; the Jacobite church, whose members are chiefly in Syria and Iraq with a Patriarch in Antioch; and the Coptic Church, which is under the Patriarch of Alexandria who also has authority over the Monophysite Church of Abyssinia (Ethiopia).

There are about 2,000 Protestants in Israel, and there are various types of Protestant churches throughout the Holy Land.

Oil tanker in Eilat   Marble quarry near Acre

THE ECONOMY From the economic point of view,
Israel is physically poor. It has neither water power,
coal, nor natural forests; only a little proven gas and
oil, few minerals, and limited farmlands. Its main
assets are the fertile soil on which its oranges are
grown, and the potash and other deposits of the South.

But history has brought about a rapid expansion of
the country's economy. Over a million immigrants have
had to be fed, housed, and clothed, and a great effort
has been made to achieve economic self-sufficiency.
Contributions from Jewish communities abroad, loans
from foreign governments, and reparations from Germany have helped to cover the deficit in the balance
of trade. Exports have greatly increased. Among the
main products sold abroad are phosphates, potash,
industrial diamonds, citrus fruits, textiles, bananas, ply-
wood, plastics, and eggs. Transport is a major part
of the country's economy. The merchant fleet has more
than 90 ocean-going vessels. The El Al Israel Airlines
carry over half of all air passengers to and from Israel.

National Water Carrier from the Sea of Galilee to the Negev Desert

By draining swamps, anchoring sand dunes with special vegetation, improving the soil, combating erosion, and finding new sources of water, Israel has cultivated over a million acres of land, with almost a third of this area irrigated. The most important water project is the National Water Carrier, which brings water from the Sea of Galilee to the Negev. There are desalination plants at Eilat and on the Mediterranean.

Among the new industrial crops introduced in Israel, the most successful are cotton, peanuts, and sugar beets. More than three-quarters of the country's food is now locally grown. Oil wells provide about a tenth of the country's oil needs. Imported oil is piped from Eilat to refineries in Haifa. There are important cement works, notably at Ramla. The economy is a mixture of private, state-owned, and cooperative enterprises. The *Histadrut*, Israel's General Federation of Labor, is at the same time a federation of trade unions and of social welfare associations, an educational agency, and an owner of, or partner in, many economic enterprises.

Pastoral scene near Mt. Tabor   Trucking oranges to Haifa

AGRICULTURE has largely become modernized. Land reclamation has taken three main forms: draining swamps, terracing, and soil conservation in the Negev and on the creeping coastal dunes. Drainage of the last and largest swamp area, the Huleh Valley, was completed in 1958; 15,000 acres of land were redeemed. The lowering of the ground water table has improved the quality of another 15,000 acres in the valley, and permitted good crops of cotton, corn, wheat, peanuts, and flower bulbs. Nearly 100,000 acres of hilly tracts, chiefly in the Upper Galilee and the Judean Hills, have been reclaimed by blasting out the rocks, gathering the stones, and terracing. In the Negev, contour plowing, closing deep gullies, and planting shelter belts have pushed back the desert for more than forty miles.

The cultivation and export of flowers has become an important industry, utilizing Israel's abundant sunlight and mild winters. Between December and April, hundreds of thousands of flowers are flown to Europe. Tulip bulbs, grown under Israel's favorable conditions, are transplanted to bloom in Holland.

Agave is grown for its fibers.   Arab farmer using tractor

CITRUS is Israel's most important agricultural crop. About three quarters of the citrus yield is exported, mainly to Europe. Groves cover an area of over 100,000 acres throughout the country, except in the hilly regions and in the deep Negev, where there are only a few experimental citrus farms.

The sweet orange (called the "golden apple" in Hebrew) is modern Israel's most popular fruit. The Shamouti orange, native of Palestine, probably takes its name from the Arabic word for a barrel-shaped oil lamp, which the fruit resembles. Israel is the world's second largest producer of grapefruit. The lemon, the sour orange, and the lime were already found in Palestine at the time of the Crusades. But the variety chiefly grown in Israel is the Eureka lemon, first developed in California from Sicilian seeds, originating from the Himalayas. The Clementine tangerine is also grown (it was developed in Algeria by a Trappist monk, a Brother Clement). The shaddock (or pummelo), the largest of all citrus fruit, is sometimes as much as 10 inches in diameter; Israelis call it the Goliath.

Kibbutz school children   Kibbutz-grown flowers

THE KIBBUTZ, in Hebrew, means "group." But during the past 50 years, the word has acquired a special meaning. Israel's 230 *kibbutzim,* or voluntary collective settlements, together with a network of farming villages *(moshavim),* form the backbone of the country's agriculture. They have made a striking contribution to Israel's development. The first *kibbutzim* were established at the turn of the century to reclaim and guard the land, in the form of small pioneering communities based on full economic equality and dedicated to manual labor and working the soil.

The land of the *kibbutzim* is owned by the Jewish National Fund. A central organization provides the initial tools, livestock, seeds, and building materials for new settlements. No *kibbutz* member is paid for working, but receives housing, clothing, medical services, books, pocket-money, and food in a communal dining hall which is also the social center. Children attend *kibbutz* schools. The standard of living varies with the financial state of the *kibbutzim,* some of which own thriving factories or fishing fleets. Many of them have

Animal corner in kibbutz   Nahal soldier on patrol

guest houses for tourists, and some even have hotels.

The *Moshav Ovdim* (workers' cooperative village) is another system of group living unique to Israel. It is more popular nowadays than the *kibbutz* among new immigrants because *moshav* members live with their own families, in their own houses, and work their own land. Heavy farm equipment is shared and the produce is marketed collectively.

The *Nahal* (from the Hebrew initials for "Pioneer Fighting Youth") is yet another system, combining military service with agricultural work. It is operated by a special section of the Israel Defense Force (into which both women and men are conscripted) in the most dangerous parts of Israel. At 18, all Israelis are drafted for two years. Those who opt for *Nahal* spend the first few months in intensive military training as a group, then a few months in an established *kibbutz*. Finally, and still together, the groups join a frontier settlement, chiefly in mountainous or desert areas still too exposed for civilians. After their service, many *Nahal* youngsters remain on the frontiers to form new *kibbutzim*.

MANDELBAUM GATE was the famous crossing point between Israeli and Jordanian sectors of Jerusalem.

CITIES AND SITES

JERUSALEM Inhabited since the beginning of the Old Stone Age, and occupied 3,000 years ago by King David whose fortress capital it became, Jerusalem perches 2,500 feet above the sea in the bare Judean hills. Its Canaanite name was Yerushalayim, and it is called El Quds—the holy—in Arabic. Always a city of contention, coveted, besieged, and often conquered, Jerusalem was divided until June, 1967.

Sacred to three faiths, Jerusalem is the capital of Israel. The modern Israeli city (pop. 200,000) was built in the last hundred years and lies west of the Old City (pop. 100,000). Scores of churches, synagogues, and mosques attest to Jerusalem's unique spiritual character.

JERUSALEM On the opposite page, the city in the 15th century, from an illuminated manuscript. In the foreground, an abandoned castle, probably Ath- lit. Then, Ramla with its mina-rets. In the walled city, Dome of the Rock, and Holy Sepulchre (with open-top dome). Top left, Mount of Olives.

91

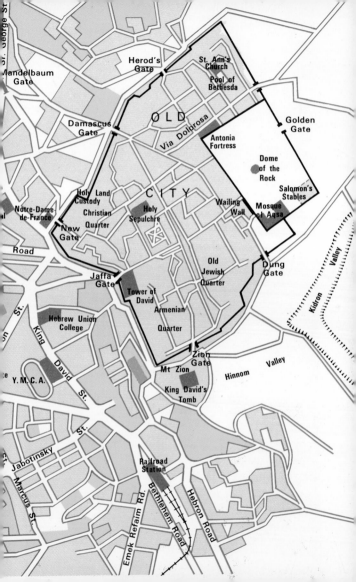

JERUSALEM, New City, seen from the south

BENEDICTINE monastery of the Dormition where, according to Christian tradition, the Virgin Mary fell into eternal sleep

MOUNT ZION, with the old windmill of Yemin Moshe Montefiore, the oldest Jewish settlement outside the city walls. At right is the rotunda of the Monastery of the Dormition, built at the beginning of the century on ground given by the Turkish Sultan to the German Kaiser.

COENACULUM, in the top story of the building which is said to contain the tomb of David, is the Hall of the Last Supper where Jesus and the Disciples celebrated the first night of the Passover and instituted the rite of the Eucharist.

EIN KAREM, just west of Jerusalem, is a pretty hamlet where, according to tradition, St. John the Baptist was born to the High Priest Zacharias and his wife Elizabeth. A prophet in the tradition of Elijah, John preached and lived in the desert near the Dead Sea, ate locusts and wild honey, and wore a garment of rough camel's hair. Ein Karem means the Spring of the Vineyard. The Church of St. John, above right, is Russian Orthodox.

MONASTERY OF THE CROSS belongs to the Greek Orthodox Church. The legend is that the tree from which the cross was fashioned for the crucifixion of Jesus grew here. In the Middle Ages, the monastery was owned by Georgians from Southern Russia.

RUSSIAN CATHEDRAL, in the Russian Compound which once housed the Russian pilgrims to the Holy Land, stands where the Assyrians camped when they lay siege to Jerusalem in 700 B.C. On the same site the Romans prepared for the assault on the city in A.D. 70.

SANHEDRIA is the burial place of the Sanhedrin, the supreme court of Israel in ancient times, whose 72 members sat in judgment in the Temple area. At right is one of the entrances to the necropolis. Below are the tombs cut in the rock.

Another ancient site in the New City is Herod's family tomb, near the King David Hotel, a mausoleum of huge stone blocks, closed by a stone door whose hinges are also cut from stone. Herod's own tomb is near Bethlehem. A monument of the Herodian period was discovered in the center of the Russian compound built by Tsarist Russia in the center of New Jerusalem: it is a huge broken column, believed to be one of the columns for the Herodian temple which was destroyed by the soldiers of Titus in A.D. 70.

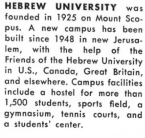

JERUSALEM

HEBREW UNIVERSITY was founded in 1925 on Mount Scopus. A new campus has been built since 1948 in new Jerusalem, with the help of the Friends of the Hebrew University in U.S., Canada, Great Britain, and elsewhere. Campus facilities include a hostel for more than 1,500 students, sports field, a gymnasium, tennis courts, and a students' center.

UNIVERSITY has an enrollment of about 12,000 from all continents. Israeli students, both boys and girls, serve in the Army between high school and university. The Medical School has been set up by Hadassah; the World Health Organization helped organize courses for students from the developing countries. In the floor of the Administration building, a beautiful 15th century mosaic found in the Valley of Jezreel has been set. The University offers degrees in humanities, Jewish, African, and Asian studies, life sciences, physics, mathematics, law, and medicine.

JERUSALEM with its cool mountain weather is known as a pleasant summer resort. The city's planning department has decreed that all new buildings should be built or faced with pink-gold Jerusalem sandstone, and the modern city has a handsome beauty and dignity of its own. Here, the well-kept Jerusalem Municipal Park.

THE NEW AND THE OLD

YAD VASHEM is the National Monument to the six million Jews of Europe killed by the Nazis during World War II. Literally, it means "hand and name"; figuratively, "monument and memorial." The square building of uncut boulders contains an eternal flame, archives, an exhibition hall, and a record of all known names of those who were killed.

MEA SHEARIM is the old quarter of the city, established in 1875, where Orthodox East European Jews have preserved the customs of their ghettos abroad. They speak Yiddish, believing that Hebrew should be reserved for prayers and sacred reading. One small group of ultra-orthodox Jews calls itself "Guardians of the City" and even refuses to recognize the authority of the state. The cobbled lanes, dark synagogues, and small houses seem to be of another century. Driving a car in the old quarter on Saturday is not recommended, as it is considered to be a desecration of the Sabbath.

MARKET PLACE in the old quarter is frequented chiefly by strictly observant Russian and Polish Jews. Men wear beards and side curls because the Bible forbids shaving, and dress in black coats and fur hats on Sabbath and holy days. Their way of life is devoted to study and prayer, and many view modern Israelis and tourists with scorn.

VIEW OF OLD CITY from Notre Dame Monastery terrace. **1)** Mount Scopus and the old Hebrew University campus; **2)** Jericho road outside of the walls; **3)** the Damascus Gate; **4)**

JERUSALEM—THE OLD CITY

History is nowhere crammed into so small an area as in the walled Old City of Jerusalem. Within this one square mile, Abraham offered Isaac to the Lord, David reigned and Solomon built the Temple, Jesus preached and was sentenced to die on the cross, and Mohammed is believed to have ascended to heaven.

Egyptian hieroglyphics dated to 2000-1900 B.C. mention the name of a town which was interpreted as Urusalim, a name which reappears in 14th century B.C. in diplomatic archives of Amen-hotep IV. The name Urusalim may originate from the same root as the Arabic Salam (the Hebrew Shalom), "peace be with you."

Jerusalem was one of the last cities to be conquered by the Israelites. It is a strong point where the native Jebusites, probably supported by the Philistine sea-people, resisted until about 1000 B.C. The city was taken by stratagem, when some of David's soldiers entered it through a water tunnel.

Augusta Victoria Hospice; **5)** Mount of Olives; **6)** Garden of Gethsemane; **7)** Pater Noster Church; **8)** Dome of the Rock. The Holy Sepulchre and Calvary are outside of the picture.

Strategically situated between lands conquered by the tribes, Jerusalem became the capital of David's Kingdom and later the Kingdom of Judah. In 701 B.C. Jerusalem was besieged but saved by a plague among Assyrian soldiers. When the city fell to the Babylonians in 587 B.C., many Jews were exiled and some returned after 538 B.C., when Cyrus of Persia became the master of the world. Jerusalem's next master was Alexander the Great. In 167 B.C., a Syrian army of Antiochus was garrisoned there. A few years later "guerillas" (notably, Judas Maccabee) drove out the Syrians. The Romans took over in 63 B.C.

Today, the Old City on Mount Moriah is enclosed by a well-preserved crenelated wall built under the Turkish Sultan, Suleiman II, in 1538. It has seven gates: the Jaffa Gate to the west; the Golden Gate in the east; the New Gate, Damascus Gate, and Herod's Gate on the north; the Zion Gate and the Dung Gate on the south. Inside, there is a tangle of narrow streets and dark arcades, a jumble of stone houses, and sites holy to three religions.

The arrival of Pope Paul VI at the Damascus Gate in Jerusalem, January 4, 1964

Jesus went to Jerusalem at the beginning of his ministry, probably in A.D. 28. He healed the sick, and spoke in the court of the Temple.

When Jesus returned to Jerusalem in A.D. 29, it was a triumphal entrance. He went to the Temple, drove out the money changers and the merchants, and for the next few days preached in Jerusalem, returning to Bethany at night.

Traditionally, the Last Supper took place in a house in the southwestern corner of the city. From there Jesus went to the Mount of Olives, stopping in the small garden of Gethsemane, where He was arrested and taken to the High Priest's palace, to the palace of the Roman Governor, and then to Herod's Palace, all within the city walls.

Herod Antipas, who ruled Galilee under Roman

The Mount of Olives, Garden of Gethsemane, and the Basilica of the Agony

supervision, mockingly ordered Jesus to be sent to Pontius Pilate, the Roman Governor, who condemned Him to death by crucifixion. That night Jesus was kept in the Antonia Fortress, where He was whipped. The pavement of the fortress has since been uncovered by archeologists and marks which may have been made on the stones for the "King's Game," such as was played by the soldiers guarding Him, have been identified.

In the morning Jesus was taken along what is now known as the Via Dolorosa to the Hill of Golgotha (the skull), and crucified. This was outside the city's limits, so that the church of the Holy Sepulchre, built and rebuilt several times throughout the centuries, may not actually be on the site of the crucifixion. The location of the garden of Joseph of Arimathea, where the body of Jesus was buried, has not been ascertained.

VIA DOLOROSA, the path of Jesus from the Antonia Fortress to Calvary, is a term which came into use in the 16th century. The path is followed by pious Christians every Friday, particularly during Holy Week (above), with stops at the Fourteen Stations of the Cross, established by tradition since the 15th century. The first station, *Condemnation*, is in the courtyard of an Arab school, and the last at the Holy Sepulchre.

ST. ANNE'S CHURCH is the most beautiful Crusader church in the Holy Land, located on the site of a Roman villa. It was first named for the Virgin Mary, and originally built on the supposed site of the house of Joachim and Anne, the birthplace of the Virgin. Later renamed for St. Anne, it was turned by Saladin into a school for dervishes. The archway shown here is an example of the church's unusual architecture.

THE HOLY SEPULCHRE, a church originally built on the site believed to be that of Mount Calvary, where Jesus died on the cross, is a patchwork of restorations and additions. In its rotunda is the small shrine which covers the traditional site of Jesus' tomb; it is the Chapel of St. Helena, Emperor Constantine's mother, who came to Jerusalem in 326 in search for the "true cross," which she is said to have found on this spot. Several chapels and churches have been erected around the site of the tomb, and a Jewish burial chamber is said to contain the body of Joseph of Arimathea.

GETHSEMANE The Franciscan Church of Gethsemane, or "Church of All Nations," is new, but erected where once stood a 4th century basilica. Behind it is the Garden of Gethsemane (meaning "the oil press") where Jesus was betrayed by Judas, and where violets and cyclamen still bloom, under gnarled olive trees. The ancient trees still standing today do not date from the time of Christ, but may have grown from shoots of trees cut down by Titus' soldiers. (At the time of the Arab conquest of Palestine, the Garden of Gethsemane, a religious shrine, was exempt from the tax on olive trees.) Above is the Russian convent of St. Magdalena. The Mount of Olives (2,680 ft. above sea level) is topped with a cluster of churches and convents; also galleries known as the Tombs of the Prophets and venerated by Jews as the tombs of Zechariah, Malachi, and Haggai.

Calvary is a platform, reached by steps built in 1810. The Chapel of Golgotha was once covered with mosaics, of which only fragments remain. It was believed in the third century that Adam had been buried in the Calvary and that his skull was discovered when Christ died (hence the name of Golgotha, "the place of the skull").

The Holy Sepulchre is shared by representatives of most of the churches of Christendom. During Holy Week it offers a range of Christian ceremonial seen nowhere else in the world.

THE CITY of Jerusalem was a stronghold of the Jebusites in the Bronze Age until captured by David about 1000 B.C. It was the seat of the Jewish kingdom until it was destroyed by the Babylonians in 586 B.C., and a wealthy capital under the Herods. It was destroyed by Titus in A.D. 70, and replaced by a city built by Hadrian in the second century A.D. The walls that surround the Old City today were built largely under Suleiman the Magnificent in the 16th century—and they are generally located north of the Herodian walls.

East of the walls lies the Valley of Kidron, separating Jerusalem from the Mount of Olives. Jesus crossed the valley with His Disciples after the Last Supper, on His way to the Garden of Gethsemane, where He was arrested. South of the Old City walls is the Valley of Hinnom (from which comes the word Gehenna, meaning Hell) across which runs the road south to Bethlehem.

Among the many monuments in the Old City, some of the most famous are, in addition to those cited above, the Mosque of Aksa, believed to have been built as a basilica by Justinian in A.D. 536, and partly disfigured by restoration in 1938. It contains the tombs of the assassins of Thomas á Becket, who joined the Knights Templar after the murder. The citadel known as David's Tower, which incorporates the ruins of the palace of Herod the Great, was in fact erected hundreds of years after David.

The Wailing Wall

The Dome of the Rock

THE DOME OF THE ROCK   The southeast corner of the Old City is taken up by a stone courtyard, in the center of which stands the Dome of the Rock, or Mosque of Omar, one of the world's most beautiful religious structures. Octagonal in shape, crowned by a great golden dome, it is decorated with Persian tiles that glow green, blue, and gold. Every day, and particularly on Friday, faithful Moslems flock to pray near and in the mosque.

It was completed in A.D. 691 over the rock on which Abraham is said to have readied his son for sacrifice, and from which Moslems believe Mohammed to have been transported to heaven on his black steed. To the east of this site, Solomon had built his Temple. Part of the Western wall of the courtyard still stands—the Wailing Wall where Jews traditionally assemble to mourn the Temple's destruction. Nearby was Pilate's palace and the Judgment Hall from which Jesus walked along the Fourteen Stations of the Cross.

HEBRON, some 30 miles south of Jerusalem, is believed to be one of the oldest towns in the world. Abraham purchased the Cave of Machpelah in Hebron to serve as a burial place for his wife, Sarah. Abraham, Isaac, Rebecca, and Jacob were later buried in the Cave, now known as the Tomb of the Patriarchs, above which a mosque, Haram el Khalil, has been erected. Joshua sacked the town and slaughtered its inhabitants. David was crowned King in Hebron after the death of Saul and ruled from it for seven years, until the conquest of Jerusalem.

The town was sacked again by Judas Maccabee, and by Titus' soldiers. A bishopric in 1168, it became Moslem in 1187. Hebronites revolted in 1834, but were defeated by Ibrahim Pasha, who destroyed part of the town. It was occupied by Allenby in 1917, and by the Israel Defence Forces fifty years later. The modern town, El Khabil in Arabic, has some 35,000 inhabitants.

JACOB'S WELL Some 40 miles north of Jerusalem on the road to Nablus is Jacob's Well, said to have been dug by the Patriarchs. Here Jesus may have stopped to talk to the Samaritan woman about the Water of Life.

BAPTISMAL CHAPEL is by the Jordan as it nears the Dead Sea, where John the Baptist performed baptismal rites. A chapel has been erected near the place where, traditionally, Jesus Himself received the baptism.

BETHANY, above, is a small Arab village near the Mount of Olives. Jesus often stayed here in the house of Martha and Mary, and supped in the home of Simon the Leper. Bethany is a contraction of Beth Anania, the name of the village when it belonged to the tribe of Benjamin.

BETHLEHEM is less than 10 miles south of Jerusalem. It is a town of some 20,000, mostly Christians. The birthplace of Jesus and of King David is called Beit Lahm (house of meat) in Arabic, and Beit Lehem (house of bread) in Hebrew. The site of the idyl of Ruth and Boaz, it is one of the holiest Christian sites. A Basilica of the Nativity (above right) was erected by Constantine in the 4th century. It was transformed by Justinian in the 6th century, and escaped Persian destruction in 614 because the invaders recognized their national costume, worn by a Magi, represented on a mosaic. Restored many times, the Basilica is centered on the Grotto of the Nativity (right), a crypt with a star covering the traditional site of the birth of Jesus. (Because of errors in the Christian calendar, it is now believed that the date of the birth of Jesus is 6 B.C.)

NORTHERN ISRAEL

NAZARETH In the heart of the Galilean mountains, Nazareth (population 30,000), the childhood home of Jesus, is one of the fairest towns in Galilee. From 1099 on it was the Crusader capital of Galilee for many years. In 1263 Nazareth was captured, largely destroyed by the Moslems, and slept away the centuries until it became the administrative center of Galilee during the British Mandate.

Today it is Israel's largest Arab city and the heart of Israel's Christian community. Nazareth has over thirty churches and monasteries, of which the newest is the basilica being built on the 13th century site of the Crusader Church of the Annunciation. Steps lead down to its grotto where, according to Christian tradition, the Angel Gabriel appeared to Mary and announced the birth of Jesus. Nearby is the Church of Joseph built over the cave where Mary and Joseph are believed to have lived.

Basilica of the Annunciation

Mary's Well

NAZARETH A panoramic view of Kiryat Natzrat in the background. showing the growing new city

The "Synagogue Church" is a Greek Catholic parish church which stands, according to tradition, on the site of the synagogue which Jesus attended and where He began to teach. Not far away is Mensa Christi, the small Franciscan Church which contains the rock called "The Table of Christ" where Jesus is believed to have supped with His Disciples after the Resurrection.

By the side of the road to Tiberias is Mary's Well, known also as the Virgin's Fountain, where Arab women carrying earthen jars still gather at dusk as they did 2,000 years ago, when Jesus and Mary drew water from it. On the mountain overlooking Nazareth is one of Israel's most beautiful churches, the Church of the Infant Jesus. The Convent of Mary's Fear, where Mary watched an angry Nazarene crowd drive Jesus to the precipice after He had preached in a local synagogue, is in the southern section of the city, near a rocky slope with a projecting ridge from which Jesus was to be cast. A Maronite church stands at the foot of the ridge.

KFAR KANA, four miles northeast of Nazareth, is a picturesque Arab village. It is the traditional site of Jesus' first miracle, the transformation of water into wine. Today, two churches (one Greek Orthodox, the other Franciscan) commemorate the Miracle of the Wedding of Cana. At the edge of the little village, the spring still bubbles from which that water came. Above left, the Franciscan church, with the Chapel of St. Nathanael in the foreground. At right is a monument erected on the site believed to be Mary Magdalene's birthplace.

THE SEA OF GALILEE, or Lake Tiberias, is called Kinneret in Hebrew, from the word *Kinor,* or harp, which the ancient Jews thought it resembled. In the New Testament, it is mentioned as the Sea of Gennesaret. Thirteen miles long and five miles wide near Tiberias, it lies 680 feet below sea level and is fed partly by natural springs, most of its water coming from the Jordan River which enters the sea near Chorazin, where Jesus once preached. A few miles north of Tiberias are the ruins of Magdala (now Migdal) where Mary Magdalene was born, and beyond it are the eucalyptus groves of Tabgha, where tradition has it that Jesus miraculously fed the multitudes. Nearby are the giant pipes and pumps of Israel's National Water Carrier.

Jesus began His public life on the shores of Galilee, and according to the Gospel of St. John, revealed Himself there to some of the Disciples after the Resurrection.

AT TABGHA is the 4th century Church of the Multiplication of the Loaves and Fishes, with a magnificent Byzantine mosaic floor depicting birds and plants that once existed in the Huleh Valley. Above Tabgha is the Mount of the Beatitudes where Jesus preached the Sermon on the Mount, and chose His Apostles. The black basalt Church of the Beatitudes was built by the Franciscans in 1937. Farther along the northern shore is Capernaum (Kfar Nahum in Hebrew) where Jesus lived when He left Nazareth, and where He met Simon and Andrew.

Ein Gev, near the Syrian border, which can only be reached by road from the south, or by ferry boat from Tiberias, is a fishing village where an international music festival is held each spring. Rising above it is a 600-foot hill, Susita, where remains have been found of 5th and 6th century streets and churches.

CAPERNAUM is along the shore of the Sea of Galilee near Tiberias. The synagogue, partly restored in the 1st or 2nd century A.D., is said to be on the site where Jesus often taught.

MOUNT OF BEATITUDES above Tabgha, is also site of Christ's preaching. Shown here is Pope Paul VI during his visit to the Holy Land, in the Italian-style Church of the Beatitudes.

TIBERIAS lies halfway along the western shore of the Sea of Galilee, 682 feet below sea level, a winter resort since the days when rich Romans sunned themselves there. It was built in A.D. 20 by one of the sons of Herod the Great and named after the Roman Emperor Tiberius. Just south of Tiberias, the famous hot springs, now known to be radioactive, have been used for medical purposes for over 2,000 years.

After the fall of Jerusalem and the repression of the Jewish uprising led by Bar Kochba in A.D. 135, most of the Jews remaining in Palestine lived in the Galilee. Great rabbinical schools grew up throughout the area and much of the Talmud was completed in Tiberias. Between the 2nd and 5th centuries the city served as the administrative and religious center of the Jews in Galilee. Under early Moslem rule Tiberias flourished but the Crusader wars drove away many Jewish inhabitants.

SEA OF GALILEE is entirely in Israel. It is a peaceful, beautiful lake, seen here as it may have appeared after Jesus calmed its waters during a storm or after the miraculous hauling of fish.

TIBERIAS today is a flourishing modern city and a favorite year-round vacation resort for Israeli and foreign tourists. It faces Ein Gev and the hills of Syria across the Sea of Galilee.

Tiberias drifted into torpor again, but in the Middle Ages, hundreds of Jews expelled from Spain in 1492 made it their home. In 1560, Suleiman the Magnificent, Sultan of the Turkish Empire, gave Tiberias a Jewish advisor, Don Joseph Nassi, the Duke of Naxos, who tried unsuccessfully to turn it into a Jewish city-state.

The great Jewish medieval scholar and physician, Maimonides, (known also, from his Hebrew initials, as the Rambam) who died in Egypt, is buried in Tiberias, as are many other famous sages. The lower city, which faces the sea, is built largely of the black basalt characteristic of Galilee, and ruins of Crusader and Turkish fortifications still stand in the streets. With its new urban housing projects on the slope above the old city, Tiberias has a population of over 20,000. Several Christian hospices are located in Tiberias; modern hotels have been built in and near the town.

SAFAD The interior of this ancient synagogue was brought from Italy.

HULEH NATURE RESERVE, with pelicans at lower left.

THE HULEH VALLEY Before the State of Israel was established, much of the triangular, 15-mile long valley in the northeastern corner of the country was covered by a malarial swamp and a muddy lake. In this valley three streams merge to form the Jordan River, and the 15,000 water-logged acres were created when prehistoric volcanic eruptions poured lava into the valley, damming the Jordan in its descent to the Sea of Galilee.

Since the proclamation of the State, more than 4 million cubic yards of earth have been dug out, dense masses of papyrus and lotus have been uprooted, and canals have been dug, criss-crossing the area. Dams and sluices have been installed to keep the water moving and prevent the breeding of malarial mosquitoes. On the land which was redeemed, the Huleh Valley Authority now directs the farming of maize, wheat, cotton, rice, sugar cane, and flower bulbs. Eight thousand acres have been set aside as a nature reserve and sanctuary.

SAFAD, 2,800 feet above sea level, is the northern-most and highest city in Israel. Above it rises Mount Canaan (3,149 feet), and beyond it stand the twin peaks of Mount Meron (or Atzmon) at 3,692 feet.

On the heights of Safad was a beacon, part of a chain of lights starting in Jerusalem and used by 2nd and 3rd century Jews to signal the beginning of each new month and holidays. In the 16th century, Safad was the center of Cabalism, the mystical interpretation of the Scriptures, and a focal point of Jewish learning. The first printing press in Asia was set up there in 1577, and the first Hebrew book printed in 1578. In the course of centuries, Safad suffered from locusts, plagues, and earthquakes that decimated its population time and again. Romans, Crusaders, Mamelukes, Arabs, and the Druse all fought for its possession.

Safad's climate makes it a popular summer resort. Safad's magic is still in its twisted alleys and the dim graveyards of the medieval mystics buried there. Scores of ruined synagogues on the hills around the town attest to its former glory. Each spring, pious Jews come to the grave of Rabbi Bar Yohai, who taught in the 2nd century, to celebrate his ascent to paradise, and at sun-down the heights are lit again by the beacons.

Artists' quarter in Safad overlooks the town.

MOUNT TABOR (1929 ft.) is an important Old Testament site, where northern tribes of Israel rallied against the Canaanites. It is the traditional site of the transfiguration of Jesus. The Franciscan Monastery serves as a hospice for pilgrims. In background at left, the Basilica of the Transfiguration.

ARAB VILLAGE of Daburiya on the road to Mt. Tabor

THE JORDAN RIVER is seen here in Upper Galilee. A small stream with a long history, it starts with three tributaries at the foot of Mt. Hermon in Lebanon, and ends at the northern shore of the Dead Sea. It is now used for irrigation.

WESTERN GALILEE An Arab shepherd and his flock, a scene that has not changed since the time of David

St. JOHN'S CRYPT in Acre, recently excavated under the Turkish citadel, was probably refectory of Hospitaler knights. An underground passage to the sea permitted the knights to reach the harbor directly, even during a siege.

ACRE Acre's history goes back to the Middle Bronze Age. It is called Akko in the Old Testament. The Greeks knew it as Ptolemais, and as such it is mentioned in the New Testament. The Crusaders fortified it and turned it into a seaport for the Christian kingdom. As the headquarters of the Order of the Knights of St. Jean d'Acre, during the Crusades, it was renamed for their patron saint.

It remained the Crusader capital from 1192 until 1291 when the fortress was recaptured by the Moslems, ending Crusader rule in Palestine. Acre declined gradually until 1775, when it became the seat of the Turkish governors, notably Ahmed el Jazzar, who built Acre's Turkish walls, the bathhouse and mosque, all of which, to this day, give the city its special and exotic character.

Today it is one of the largest cities in Israel with a mixed Arab-Jewish population.

HAIFA is Israel's second largest city and main port, and the center of the country's heavy industry. Located at the meeting place of mountain, valley, and sea, it climbs the slopes of lovely Mount Carmel. Haifa is not mentioned at all in the Bible, but its name appears in Jewish Talmudic literature of the 3rd century A.D. The Crusaders who captured it called it Caiphas.

Under Moslem rule, Haifa prospered but by the time of the Turks it had become an unimportant village. It began to develop at the beginning of the 20th century. The harbor is equipped to handle 2,500,000 tons of cargo a year and is the home base of Israel's navy and merchant fleet. Beautiful Haifa Bay is the site of oil refineries, a foundry, glass and textile works, and various chemical industries.

To the east, are several Druse villages, and one village, Kababir, still within the boundaries of Haifa, is populated by members of the Ahmadia sect, founded in India.

Ein Hod, some miles south of Haifa, is an artist's colony and the home of many of Israel's painters and sculptors.

Panorama of Haifa and its busy port

TECHNION CITY, the 300-acre campus on Mount Carmel of the Israel Institute of Technology

The city itself is built on three levels. The old Lower Town around the harbor is known as Hadar Hacarmel ("The Glory of Carmel"). Above it is Haifa's commercial center, which contains museums of antiquities, ethnology, Japanese art, and a Maritime Museum known for its collection of ancient maps and ship models. The highest level is Mount Carmel. The slopes of the mountain are dominated by the Bahai Temple surrounded by a Persian Garden, and residential suburbs along the mountain top. A subway starts near the port and travels up Mount Carmel in a tunnel bored through the rock.

The French Carmel on the western promontory is, according to tradition, where the Prophet Elijah taught his disciples. Above Elijah's cave stands a Carmelite Monastery which was used as a hospital by Bonaparte in 1799; the soldiers who died there are buried at the entrance. Next to it is the Stella Maris lighthouse from which one can see to the north, beyond the Lebanese border, the cliffs of the Ladder of Tyre, an assault embankment constructed by Alexander the Great in 332 B.C. Inland from Athlit, in the foohills of the Carmel, are the caves where several complete prehistoric skeletons and Stone Age implements have been excavated.

ATHLIT Unlike most of the great Crusader castles in the Holy Land, the Templar Castle of the Pilgrims, or Chateau Pelerin, at Athlit, eight miles south of Haifa, was never taken by siege. The last Christian stronghold in the Holy Land, and a chief port of

Crusader walls of Athlit

entry for Christian pilgrims in the Middle Ages, the Castle was intact when it was abandoned without a battle in 1291, shortly after the fall of Acre. But the Moslems, probably fearing new invasions from Europe, largely destroyed it. An earthquake in 1837 added to the destruction, but even today, the ruins of the walls of Athlit are an impressive reminder of Crusader might.

Knights' Hall in Templar Castle

CAESAREA A Roman aqueduct, recently dug out from the sand, was used to supply water from the north. At right are ruins of Crusader fortifications, built with Roman columns.

CAESAREA   Contrasts abound at Caesarea. A many-arched Roman aqueduct, a first century hippodrome, a Crusader moat, a 19th century mosque, and a 20th century *kibbutz* jostle each other on this small stretch of coast halfway between Tel Aviv and Haifa. Caesarea was buried under the drifting sands hundreds of years ago, but recent archeological excavations have uncovered fabulous landmarks, including an Herodian harbor, the only known engraved stone bearing the name of Pontius Pilate, Roman statues, remnants of a Crusader citadel, a Byzantine church with mosaics of birds and animals, and a 4th century synagogue.

Founded as a port in 22 B.C. by King Herod the Great, Caesarea was named for the Roman Emperor Augustus Caesar. For 300 years it was the magnificent capital of the Roman procurators in Palestine. Caesarea was a center of Jewish revolt, later became an important center of rising Christianity, and is mentioned several times in the Acts of the Apostles. It was for a long time one of the main ports of the Mediterranean.

St. Paul was imprisoned in Caesarea, before being sent to Rome. It was an important Byzantine stronghold, and the last to be taken by the Moslem invaders in 640, after a siege of several years. Marble and mosaic remains of 4th to 6th century synagogues have recently been unearthed. When Baldwin I captured the city during the First Crusade, he found a green crystal bowl which he believed to be the Holy Grail.

During the Crusades, the city changed hands five times. In 1251, St. Louis of France fortified Caesarea, but when the Moslems recaptured it in 1265, it was totally destroyed, and lay desolate for generations. In 1937 Sdot Yam, a cooperative fishing village, was established nearby, and after the birth of the State of Israel in 1948, large-scale restoration returned to Caesarea some of its lost splendor.

Today, it is also a vacation resort, and a center for sports. It has Israel's only 18-hole golf course, horse and camel races are held on the beach, and there is a skin-diving and underwater exploration center.

ROMAN THEATRE in Caesarea is frequently used for concerts.

CENTRAL ISRAEL

TEL AVIV (the Hill of Spring) is the world's first all-Jewish city since Biblical times. It was founded in 1909 by a handful of Jewish families who lived in Jaffa, then an Arab seaport. Tel Aviv is now the center of Israel's cultural life, the headquarters of the country's banking, trade, and light industry; with its suburbs it is Israel's largest city, housing one-sixth (over 400,000) of the country's population.

Tel Aviv is the home of nearly a dozen repertory theatres, of the National Opera Company, of almost a thousand outdoor cafes, and scores of cinemas. Twenty-five daily newspapers and periodicals in ten

Tel Aviv seashore hotels

Cafe on fashionable Dizengoff St.

languages are published and a new university is rising.

Israel's main shopping and tourist center is also the site of many government offices, of Israel's General Federation of Labor, and of the first all-Hebrew high school (on whose site now stands a 30-story skyscraper). Its main streets are Dizengoff (named for Tel Aviv's first mayor), and Allenby (for the British general who took Palestine from the Turks in 1918). Israel's Declaration of Independence was first read out in the small municipal art museum on May 14, 1948.

Accadia hotel near Tel Aviv

Even parking tickets exist in T.A.

JAFFA Now part of Tel Aviv, Jaffa is one of the oldest and most romantic seaports in the world. Its recorded history goes back 3,500 years. The Book of Chronicles mentions it as Solomon's main outlet to the sea; the Cedars of Lebanon were floated there by raft, from Tyre, and hauled to the Temple in Jerusalem. It is from here that Jonah set sail on his ill-fated voyage to Tarshish, and in Greek mythology it is probably the scene of Perseus' rescue of Andromeda from the sea monster from rocks still visible outside the harbor.

In the eighth century B.C. the Assyrians, sweeping down on the coast of Palestine from the north, conquered Philistine Jaffa.

In 332 B.C. it was taken by Alexander the Great, and in the 2nd century B.C. Judas Maccabee and his brothers fought for it and won it from the Seleucid Kingdom. Under Roman rule, Jaffa was a free city, and Mark Antony once gave it to Cleopatra as a present.

Some of the earliest Christians made their homes in Jaffa. The New Testament describes St. Peter's stay there, in the house of Simon the Tanner. Throughout the Crusades, Jaffa frequently changed hands, finally to be lost to the conquering Mameluke Sultan of Egypt, Baibars, who razed it to the ground and drove the Christians out. For a while, Jaffa prospered when Bonaparte captured it in 1799 on his way to Acre, but after a few months he abandoned it and it declined.

The first Zionist pioneers entered "the Promised Land" through Jaffa around 1840 but it remained an Arab town until the War of 1948. After the creation of the State, Tel Aviv and Jaffa officially became one, but Jaffa has kept its personality. Its population includes 60,000 Jews, and 6,500 Christian and Moslem Arabs.

OLD CITY OF JAFFA is a maze of archways, steps, terraces. The house of Simon the Tanner is said still to stand.

BRIDGE OF JINDAS built in 1273 by Baibars on foundation of older Roman bridge, near Lod, Israel's main airport.

Weizmann Institute of Science   Wine cellar in Rishon-le-Zion

RISHON-LE-ZION AND REHOVOTH   Rishon-le-Zion (The First in Zion) is typical of the small towns established throughout Israel's coastal plain by East European Zionists at the turn of the century. It was founded in 1882 by Russian Jews and was later subsidized largely by Baron Rothschild. Its winery, built in 1887, is the largest in Israel. Between the town and the coast are the sand dunes of Nahal Sorek where Israel's first atomic reactor was completed in 1960, for training and research.

Rehovoth, nearby, is the seat of the joint Hebrew University's agricultural faculty and National Agricultural Research Institute, and of the Weizmann Institute of Science, inaugurated in 1949 by Israel's first President, Dr. Chaim Weizmann, a noted chemist. The Institute, which is the most advanced center in the Middle East for research in mathematics, physics, chemistry, and biology, is located within a park which is the nation's memorial to Dr. Weizmann. Dr. Weizmann is buried in the garden of his house on the Institute's grounds.

ASHKELON, Israel's southernmost Mediterranean town, was one of the most important harbor cities in the Middle East. Captured by the Egyptian Pharaoh Rameses II in 1280 B.C., Ashkelon later became one of a confederation of five Philistine towns (with Gath, Gaza, Ashdod, and Ekron). In 732 B.C., it was captured

Crusader ruins at Ashkelon

by Tiglath Pileser III, and later came under Sennacherib, King of Assyria.

After its conquest by Alexander the Great in the 4th century B.C., Ashkelon became a Greek city. Herod the Great, who was born there, enlarged and beautified it. It was fortified in 1192 by Richard the Lion-Hearted's troops. The city fell to the Moslems in 1270, and was demolished.

Ashkelon left its mark in two English words—"shallot" and "scallion," after the onions grown there in antiquity. Recurrent legends of buried treasure led an English woman, Lady Hester Stanhope, in 1815, to excavate the site of ancient Ashkelon, in the vain hope of finding gold. Organized archeological excavations were started in 1920 and almost seven centuries after its destruction, Ashkelon was resettled.

The ancient walls and the ruins of its gates and towers are part of a large new park and camping ground near a collection of Hellenistic and Roman statues, columns, and decorated marble slabs.

Road from Beersheba to Eilat   Red Canyon in the Negev

SOUTHERN ISRAEL

THE NEGEV   Much of the 5,000-odd square miles of
southern Israel is sand, dust, eroded soil, and rock.
This area is called the Negev, and it represents more
than half of Israel's territory. The State reaches its
widest point, 70 miles, just south of Beersheba, and at
Eilat it narrows to six. Not so long ago, only the coastal
strip and the plateau of the Negev were considered
fit for cultivation, and even these were regarded as
unlikely prospects. The soil was saline. There was no
rain. The heat was extreme.

But scholars knew differently. They knew the Negev
had once sustained agriculture and industry, and that
populations of up to a hundred thousand had lived
and flourished there. King David had included the population of the Negev in a national census. Solomon
mined copper there and merchant fleets had sailed
for Africa and the Orient from the Red Sea port of
Etzion Geber. Nabateans, Arabian tradesmen, ruled

Dam believed to have been built by the Nabateans

the Negev until the Romans annexed it in A.D. 106.

The first modern assault on the Negev was made in 1943 with the establishment of three Jewish settlements, two of them *kibbutzim,* the third a small-holders' cooperative village. Each of them dug wells and found water. It was too salty to drink but the parched earth received it gladly, and the experimental crops (grains, fruit trees, forest trees, and vegetables) flourished. Rainwater was dammed and hundreds of soil samples taken. Life was rigorous, but clearly it could be sustained. In 1946, "Operation Negev" established eleven new settlements: four more followed a year later. By 1948, there were 27 villages in the Negev.

Now, there are some 200, with a total population of over 200,000. In 1955, a pipeline bringing water down from the springs of the Yarkon River to the Negev supplied some 45 million cubic meters a day. Within a decade, the giant pipes of Israel's National Water Carrier were sending over a hundred million cubic meters to the Negev from the Sea of Galilee, via the Galilee and the coastal plain.

Roman bridge, still in use   Camel mart in Beersheba

BEERSHEBA   In 1948, Beersheba, Israel's southern capital, looked almost as it had looked in Old Testament days when Abraham had "builded a tent" there and Jacob had dreamed of the ladder that reached to Heaven.

It was a dusty, battered desert town, a picturesque setting for the Bedouin who wandered through it with their flocks of sheep and camels. Reduced to a heap of rubble when it was captured by desert tribesmen from the Crusaders, Beersheba barely survived for centuries until the Turks began to use it as a center for desert trade in 1880. In World War I, Turkey lost Beersheba to the British in a climactic battle.

Today, the city is the busy hub of the Negev's economic and industrial life. It is the center of scores of industries, many based on the Negev's newly exploited raw materials; the main stop-over point to and from Eilat; and a tourist attraction in its own right. It has a typical Arab market and camel mart and a mixed Jewish-Arab population of about 60,000.

Dimona, new town in the Negev

Tourists in the desert

NEW TOWNS IN THE NEGEV A chain of new towns extending throughout the Negev hint at the scope of the attack on the seared land. The first city on the way to the Dead Sea is Dimona, which was named for a city in ancient Judah, and settled by the Dead Sea workers of Sdom. The desert is now rapidly retreating before the belts of olive trees, tamarisks, acacias, and eucalyptus which ring it. Most Dimonans work in the textile and chemical industries which have sprung up around the town.

Eight miles to the west is Kfar Yerucham near the phosphate deposits of Oron. Its founders were immigrants from Rumania, joined by others from Morocco, Iran, and Poland. Kfar Yerucham has Israel's only crystal glass works.

Mitspe-Ramon, perched over the crater which gives it its name, is at the center of the quarrying region for most of Israel's ceramic materials and gypsum. A road winds down to the crater some 400 feet below the town.

Bedouin in Beersheba   Experimental desert farm

MAN IN THE DESERT   An extensive research program is underway at Beersheba's Arid Zone Research Station where a Human Environmental Physiology Group seeks ways to help the Negev's settlers overcome the stresses of the desert climate. Another group studies the effect of aridity and the sun's scorching rays on animals. Experiments have also started at the Dead Sea Works at Sdom, and at the Timna Mines, to study the effect of heat on the working performance of acclimatized people. These experiments are continued each summer, when temperatures are extreme, reaching 100° F. in the shade, and sometimes 160° F. in the sun.

Another experiment near the Dead Sea consists of using solar energy for electricity. Results have been obtained, but the method has not yet been found applicable on a large scale. Solar heat is widely used in Israel for providing apartment houses with hot water. The climate is sunny enough the year round for water tanks on rooftops to be heated with the help of reflectors.

Arab village of Wadi Ara in the Galilee

THE BEDOUIN IN ISRAEL Of Israel's 22,000 Bedouin, some 20,600 belong to 19 tribes in the Negev. Their low black tents and tethered camels are a familiar sight throughout the South. Though some of the wealthier Sheiks have started to build stone houses, the Bedouin are still nomads. Their goathair tents, spun from shearings and woven by the women, provide protection against wind and sun, as does the black bordered head scarf or "keffiyah," kept in place by a double ring of black sheep wool known as an "agal."

The mainstay of the Bedouin diet is pittah—the traditional flat dry circular bread—sheep, goat or camel milk and cheese, dates, honey, and rice. Their staple beverage is bitter, spiced black coffee, drunk a thimbleful at a time.

Of all the progress made in Israel among the Negev Bedouin, the most striking has been in medical services and health. Thousands of tribesmen, their reticent wives, and their children have been inoculated against tuberculosis and infantile paralysis.

AVDAT A modern dance group in the restored ruins of the Nabatean city of Avdat

NABATEAN CITY seen from the air: Acropolis is in foreground. Arabic name for it was Abde.

AVDAT   Avdat, 40 miles south of Beersheba, was a Nabatean garden city on one of the major caravan routes through the Wilderness of Zin, across which the tribes of Israel had once wandered on their way to Canaan. The Nabateans (p. 132) established the city in the 3rd century B.C. Their Kingdom came to an end in A.D. 106, but Avdat lasted a thousand years.

In the middle of the 3rd century the Roman Emperor Diocletian, renewing the defenses of the Roman border, made Avdat part of a string of forts linking the Arava with the Northern Negev. The city flourished until the 6th century under Byzantine rule, but with the Moslem conquest it declined, finally to be abandoned in the 10th century.

Nearly a thousand years later, in 1949, the pioneer settlement of Sde Boker was established in the Negev and interest in the ancient and derelict city of Avdat revived. Restoration of the city was undertaken, and the ancient Nabatean channels to collect run-off water are in use once more for the growing of crops. There is a small museum with relics of the Nabatean city.

THE DEAD SEA

East of Beersheba, the Judean wilderness stretches as a plateau. Suddenly, the land drops—from 1,200 feet above sea level to 1,286 feet below sea level, to the Dead Sea, the lowest spot on the surface of the earth. Fifty miles long and nine miles wide, the Dead Sea, is part of the rift which reaches from Turkey along the Jordan River Valley to the Red Sea and into the lakes of East Africa. Still known in Hebrew by its original name, "The Sea of Salt," it is fed chiefly by the Jordan River. Because it has no outlet, its waters have evaporated for millions of years in the fiery heat, leaving behind an ever-growing residue of salt. Nothing can live in the Dead Sea except a few single-celled organisms which have adapted themselves to this unusual environment. The water contains 25% dissolved salt and other minerals, five times more than any other sea, and is so dense that no swimmer can sink. Parts of the Dead Sea are in Jordan.

The spring at Ein Gedi   Evaporating pans in Dead Sea

SDOM AND EIN GEDI   The wicked cities of the Bible, Sodom and Gomorrah, once stood near Sdom, at the southern tip of the Dead Sea. Sdom is the site of the world's largest deposit of crystalline rock salt. On a hill of salt nearby stands a pillar—traditionally Lot's wife, punished for her curiosity, forever looking back.

Modern Sdom is the location of one of Israel's most important chemical works. Potash is extracted from the Dead Sea brine, and bromine manufactured for export. From Sdom, a track runs northward along the shore to Ein Gedi, a lush green settlement in the desert, founded in 1949. Once Ein Gedi was the site of a hamlet in Judah where David the shepherd hid from Saul the King. Just beyond the settlement flows the spring known as the "Fountain of David." Ein Gedi was the only place in ancient Israel where the balsam tree flourished and it became the center of a perfume industry. Recent excavations have exposed the vessels, tools and weights used by the perfumers, and in the mountains above Ein Gedi a fortress, dated to the time of the Second Temple, has been found.

THE RED SEA   Israel and Jordan each own a few miles of the Red Sea shorefront, Israel around Eilat, and Jordan around Aqaba. The gulf is the meeting place of four countries: Egypt, Saudi Arabia, Israel, and Jordan. But the frontiers between Israel and its neighbors are closed.

For Israel, the gulf is the outlet to the Far East and to Africa; for Jordan, which has no opening to the Mediterranean, the gulf is its only access to a sea.

The gulf was one of the stations of the tribes of Israel on their way to Canaan, and an important harbor in the time of the Kingdom of Judah. Before, it was part of the Biblical Kingdom of Edom. Solomon's copper mines, on Israeli territory near Eilat, actually may have been operated before Solomon's time by Edomites. Heaps of slag testify to the activity of the mines in ancient times. The Jordanian city of Aqaba is near the ancient site of Etzion Geber, from which Solomon's fleet set sail, laden with gold for Ophir, and where the Queen of Sheba probably landed on her royal visit.

TIMNA A modern Israeli copper processing plant near the ancient "Solomon's mines"

ANCIENT copper smelting furnace may have been Edomite, preceding Solomon's time.

AQABA, Jordan's only outlet to the sea, is also being developed as a resort.

SKIN DIVING in clear waters of Red Sea may soon be spoiled by industrial developments.

EILAT AND AQABA Although Eilat and Aqaba share the shores of the Red Sea, it is impossible to go from one town to the other. They are separated by barbed wire.

The modern Israeli town of Eilat was founded in 1950. It lies 155 miles south of Beersheba, 356 miles south of Jerusalem. It has a population of several thousand, and copper is, once more, mined nearby. A few hotels have been built on the shore, and it is a favorite resort of Israeli and foreign tourists.

Aqaba, in Jordan, is the ancient city of Etzion Geber. It was known as Aila during the Crusades, when Renauld de Chatillon made it a base for looting expeditions against the Moslems, and threatened Mecca. It is also the site of one of the best known exploits of Lawrence of Arabia and his Bedouin raiders, who crossed the desert and the Edom mountains coming from the east and struck Aqaba from the rear. The Turks, taken by surprise, suffered a severe defeat.

Today, both Eilat and Aqaba are booming harbor towns, each with several tourist hotels.

THE NEIGHBORS

Arab legionnaires in Jordan

All four of the Arab countries which border on Israel have, at various times, shared a common past with it. Parts of present-day Jordan, Lebanon, Syria, and Egypt, together with Israel, formed the most important lands of the Bible. Since 1948, however, travel across the borders has often been difficult, and at times impossible. Most of the borders between Israel and the countries of Jordan, Lebanon, Syria and Egypt have been sealed for many years. But tours have been organized to visit the entire Holy Land and will doubtless be organized again. Biblical landmarks and recent archeological excavations are visited by a constantly increasing flow of travelers, and tourism is an important source of revenue to the countries which share a Biblical past.

An interesting aspect of the Arab countries bordering Israel, in addition to their archeological and religious sites, are the organized tours in the desert, the home of the Bedouin who live in goathair tents and roam the land with their camel and sheep herds. Their origin is not known; traditionally they are the descendants of Ishmael, the son of Abraham and an Egyptian concubine, Hagar. Bedouins were the "Raiders" of Lawrence of Arabia, who united to free Arabia from the Turks in 1917-18. Many of their descendants now serve in Jordan's Desert Army or the Arab Legion.

Amman, the capital of Jordan   Roman amphitheatre in Amman

JORDAN   The Hashemite Kingdom of Jordan has an area of some 37,500 square miles, and a population of over 1,850,000. It is ruled by the descendants of Hashim, believed to be Mohammed's ancestor.

Jordan's economy is less "westernized" than that of Israel, and many of the Bedouin nomads are largely unproductive, though most tribes now cultivate some land. Moreover, Jordan suffers from its isolation: its frontiers are such that it has only a small outlet to the Red Sea, at Aqaba. In the last few years, since the opening of a road from Amman to Aqaba, merchant traffic has increased, and Jordan exports phosphates, potash, wheat, dried fruit, and wool. With important religious sites and archeological excavations in Jordan, tourism is an increasingly important source of revenue.

Jordan's capital is Amman, once the city of the Ammonites. Rabbath-Ammon, as it was then called, was captured by David, and became subservient to the Kings of Samaria and of Judea. Later it fell to the Assyrians, and was Hellenized by Ptolemy II, Philadelphus, (285-247 B.C.) who called it Philadelphia.

144

One of the cities of the Greek Decapolis, Amman was part of the Nabatean Kingdom until it was conquered by Herod the Great in 31 B.C., when it became one of the outposts of the Roman Empire. An important Byzantine crossroads, it became a bishopric, then was conquered by the Moslems in 635. In 1887, a Sultan gave it to Circassians from Russia, who built their houses over (and with material from) Greco-Roman buildings that had survived until that time.

Today it has a well-preserved and restored Roman theatre, a citadel with ruins of a temple to Hercules, and an Amayyad building. The Archeological Museum houses many of the discoveries made in Jordan.

MADABA   Some 20 miles south of Amman, Madaba is known for its Byzantine mosaics, among which is a famous map of Palestine and Jerusalem, the oldest one known. The map, and other mosaics, dating to the time of Justinian (sixth century), were discovered in 1896. They were found in a Greek Orthodox Church, built on the site of a more ancient church. Near Madaba stands Mount Nebo, traditionally the summit from which Moses saw the Promised Land. There is a sweeping view of the Jordan Valley, the Dead Sea, and Jerusalem atop the mountains to the west. South through the canyon, which once served as a border between the Ammonite and Moabite tribes, stand the well-preserved remains of a major Crusader fortification, Karak and its citadel, with its many vaulted rooms and chambers and a dungeon. Recently excavated and restored, the castle is open to visitors, and a resthouse in the Crusader style has been opened in the same vault which served as a dining room for the Christian soldiers. At the summit are the remains of several early Christian churches.

Qumran Caves in which Dead Sea Scrolls were found

KHIRBET QUMRAN, near the Dead Sea a few miles west of the Jordan River, is famous as the site where most of the Dead Sea Scrolls were discovered (see page 50). Still visible are ruins of a large building believed to have been a community house of the Essenes, and grottos where some of the sectarians probably lived. Qumran is believed to have been inhabited during the first century B.C., and destroyed during an earthquake which, according to Josephus Flavius, devastated Judea during the seventh year (32-31 B.C.) of the reign of Herod the Great. Qumran was apparently resettled by the Essenes, and destroyed once more by Romans during the second Jewish uprising in A.D. 132-135. There are remnants of wells, and an Essene cemetery with more than 1000 tombs.

JERICHO One of the most important archeological sites in the world, Jericho is the oldest known city to have been lived in, perhaps without interruption, for some 10,000 years. It is near the north shore of the Dead Sea, and 825 feet below sea level.

Jericho was first occupied by a people known as the Natufians, who are believed to have come from the north, eight millenia before Christ and to have settled in the upper Jordan Valley. Natufians are believed to be the first to have known urban organization. The walls of ancient Jericho probably enclosed about eight acres, and were surrounded by a 27-foot-wide, 7-foot-deep, protective ditch. A great stone tower, 27 feet tall, with a stone stairway in its center, was erected probably between 7,000 and 6,500 B.C. There were no streets since the houses were apparently connected through courtyards. The population of Jericho may then have been as much as 3,000.

Prehistoric Jericho went through some 20 architectural phases during the 6th and 7th millenia B.C. alone. The round houses of the Natufians were followed by square and rectangular houses built by the Tahunians, nomadic tribes who resettled the city after it was abandoned by the Natufians—or who conquered it. Bones of dismembered bodies have been found, suggesting either slaughter, or burial customs.

Jericho was the first town in Canaan taken by the Israelites in the 13th century B.C. The town was sacked by Joshua, later rebuilt as part of the inheritance of Benjamin. Its population was deported to Babylonia after the invasion of Nebuchadnezzar II, and was resettled by the Jews returning from exile. Later it fell to the Syrians, then to the Romans.

Jericho was given by Mark Antony to Cleopatra,

GREAT STONE TOWER now standing at 20 ft., was probably the main lookout of the ancient citadel.

WALLS OF JERICHO surrounded the city long before Joshua blew his trumpet. In background is Mount of Temptation.

who sold it to Herod the Great. The king built a winter palace, theatre, hippodrome, and citadel. He died in Jericho in 4 B.C. It is said that on the streets of this city, Jesus healed the blind beggar, and was entertained in the house of Zaccheus, the tax collector. Even in ancient times, Jericho was a luxurious winter resort and one can still see the ornaments and mosaics of the lavish Arab palace of Caliph Hisham Ibn Abdul Malik, who ruled the Arab empire from A.D. 724-743. Today Jericho is a town of about 10,000 inhabitants.

Some two miles west of Jericho is a Greek monastery, clinging to a steep rock, the Sandarion. It was built last century over grottos, one of which has been venerated as the site where Jesus fasted for 40 days. Atop the mountain stands an ancient church, recently restored, traditionally the site of "The Temptation of Christ." There is a wall around the mountain, which is also the presumed site of the Fortress of Doch, where Simon Maccabee was assassinated in 135 B.C.

TEMPLES, funerary chapels, and homes carved in Hellenistic style from vari-colored rock are contrasted against ragged profile of pink sandstone cliffs.

PETRA became the center of the Nabatean civilization in the 4th century B.C. The Nabateans, Hellenized Arabs, spread their commercial empire from the Euphrates to Damascus and the Red Sea. They developed a new form of the Aramaic script, precursor of written Arabic.

Most of Petra's Hellenistic monuments, among the best preserved in the world, were built in the 3rd and 2nd centuries B.C.

ES SIQ, a narrow, meandering gorge, no wider than 6 to 7 feet between cliffs up to 300 feet tall, leads to the ruins of Petra, which date from the 3rd and 2nd centuries B.C. The passage was once floored with stone pavement.

North of Jerusalem are several important sites.

NABLUS, in Biblical times known as Shechem, and where Jesus talked with the woman of Samaria, is the place of worship and the site of a Samaritan temple. Nearby, on Mount Gerizim, the Samaritans still celebrate Passover by sacrificing sheep. On the road to Jerusalem are the tomb of Joseph, and Jacob's well.

SEBASTIA, a few miles northwest of Nablus, has been inhabited since the Bronze Age. It is said to be the site of the burial place of John the Baptist.

Towards Jerusalem, at El Jib, the Biblical Gideon, there is a grape press and storage chambers carved in the rock, which may be the remains of the world's oldest winery. Qubaybah is believed to be the site of ancient Emmaus, where a Franciscan church and a German hospice commemorate the visit of Jesus to the House of Cleophas after His Resurrection.

Deep into the desert west of Amman, the "desert castles" of Jordan are unique examples of Arab architecture. They were built in the 8th century to serve as hunting lodges for the Ommiad Caliphs. With a competent guide they can be reached by car or jeep. The castle of Qasr Mushatta is known for its stucco ornamentation, and that of Qasr al Smra for its wall frescoes. In the oasis of Azraq stands the castle which served as headquarters for Lawrence of Arabia during World War I.

On the heights of Ajlun (in Jordan), which rises over 4,000 ft., stands one of the few Arab castles remaining from the Crusader wars: Qal'et er-Rabad, built in 1184 by one of Saladin's emirs. Destroyed by the Mongols, it was rebuilt by Sultan Baibars, and was occupied by a Turkish Pasha until the 20th century.

Jerash—Forum, seen from the Temple of Zeus

JERASH (the Roman Gerasa) lies some 40 miles north of Amman in Jordan. It was founded as a Hellenistic town under Alexander the Great, perhaps by one of his generals, Perdiccas, and became part of the Decapolis. It fell under the influence of the Nabatean kingdom, and in the first century A.D. had all the attributes of a great Greco-Roman City: Temples, theatres, stadium, forum, baths, etc. Hadrian visited the city in A.D. 129-130, adding to its splendor. From the 4th century to the 6th, Christian Gerasa was endowed with a cathedral and a bishop, and in the 7th, it was looted by Persians and Arabs and devastated by a great earthquake.

Deserted for centuries, it was reoccupied in 1878 by Circassians who used ancient stones to build their village. Several Greco-Roman ruins have nevertheless remained in excellent condition: a triumphal arch, a stadium (with Persian polo goalposts dating to the 7th century), a forum with 56 columns still standing, a Temple of Zeus dating to the 2nd century, and a theatre for 5,000 spectators.

The Nile, with the great pyramids in the background

EGYPT The exodus of the Hebrews started from Egypt, first reaching the Sea of Reeds, at the northern end of the Red Sea, where "The Lord caused the sea to go back by a strong wind all the night, and made the sea dry land and the waters were divided." The Hebrews reached the eastern shore just in time: when the pursuing Egyptians appeared, the waters returned.

Moses then led the Hebrews through the wilderness across the Sinai Peninsula, to Mount Sinai (or Mount Horeb; probably at the place now called Djebel Musa). There he climbed the 8,000-foot mountain to receive the Ten Commandments. Moses and his people then moved northward, carrying the Ark of the Covenant, which was a box made of acacia wood, to the Promised Land.

Then they reached the Gulf of Aqaba, and moved on north (following, in fact, closely along the present-day border of Israel) to the oasis of Kadesh-Barnea, on the threshold of the Promised Land. They remained there for 38 years, until Joshua, the lieutenant of Moses, decided to start the conquest.

Egypt, from which came one of the mightiest empires of the past and one of the ancient world's greatest civilizations, today covers an area of 386,000 square miles, of which 95 per cent is desert. The country is split by the Nile River, on which its economy is based. Egypt's modern history began with its occupation by Bonaparte in 1799 and its subsequent domination by the Turks. In 1918, the Kingdom of Egypt passed into British hands, and in 1945 Egypt became independent. Following the overthrow of King Farouk in 1952, and a period of military dictatorship, Egypt was declared a republic in 1953.

The state religion is Islam and Arabic is the official language of the 29 million people who live there. English, however, is widely spoken in the cities.

Basically a farming country, Egypt's main crop is cotton. The largest cities are Cairo, the capital, and Alexandria, the principal port. Egypt's spectacular and well-preserved antiquities have made it one of the world's most fascinating countries. Vast projects have been undertaken to preserve monuments threatened by the Aswan Dam project, which is designed to bring fertility to thousands of arid acres. One of the colossal temples, Abu Simbel, has been raised, piece by piece, and assembled above the dam's projected water level. A boat trip up the Nile, Egypt's life-giving artery, is an unforgettable experience. The Cairo Museum has a large and excellent collection of antiquities.

SYRIA has been closely bound with Palestine through the ages. The country is bordered on the northwest and north by Turkey, on the east and southeast by Iraq, on the south by Jordan and Israel, and on the west by Lebanon and the Mediterranean.

Dominated in turn by the ancient Hittites, Egyptians, Assyrians, Babylonians, Persians, and Greeks, it became a Roman province in the 1st century B.C. Invaded by the Persians and afterwards by the Arabs, it was successively Turkish, Mongol, and Mameluke from the 11th to the 16th centuries. Certain regions were also occupied by the Crusaders. Until World War I, it was part of the Ottoman Empire and then came under French rule.

Syria has been independent since 1946. Today, it covers an area of some 72,250 square miles. Most of its 5,500,000 population are Arabs, of whom about 15% are Christian, the rest Moslem. Syria's largest minorities are Kurds, Armenians, and Druse. Essentially an agricultural country, it has a number of light industries. Its main towns are Damascus, the capital, Aleppo, Homs, Hama, and Latakia. Though all are ancient, Damascus has been a great town since the dawn of history, and it is mentioned in early Egyptian monuments and in the Old Testament. It was from there that Paul, traveling from Tarsus to Jerusalem on the "road to Damascus," became converted to Christianity. Damascus is one of the world's oldest cities. The Mosque of the Ommiad Caliphs, one of the architectural masterpieces of Damascus, is actually a Christian Basilica built in the 4th century A.D. on the ruins of an earlier pagan temple dedicated to Jupiter. It was used both as a Mosque and a basilica in the 7th century under the Ommiad, and was converted entirely into a mosque in the 11th century.

CEDARS OF LEBANON were used by Solomon to build his Temple. At right, the vast Temple of Jupiter at Baalbek, in Syria.

LEBANON, with 4,000 square miles, is the smallest country in the Middle East, and is named for the snow-covered Mountains of Lebanon (whose peaks rise to 10,000 feet) on which the famous cedars grew. The modern republic was formed under a French mandate in 1920 and became independent in 1946. Of Lebanon's population of 2,200,000 more than half are Christians. Lebanon has an abundant water supply and a fertile coastal plain. Three thousand years before the Christian era, this plain was occupied by the Phoenicians, the chief mariners and merchants of antiquity, whose main ports were Tyre and Sidon. Lebanon's largest city is Beirut, the capital, the home of a famous law school in the 3rd century A.D., and now the location of a great American University which has strongly influenced Arab education throughout the Middle East. Tripoli, the second largest city, is an oil pipeline terminus. Both Arabic and French are spoken in Lebanon. The ruins of a huge Roman temple at Baalbek, first named for the ancient god Baal and once known as Heliopolis, are famous. The Phoenician harbor of Byblos, once a market for papyrus, is the root of the word "Bible."

BIBLIOGRAPHY

GENERAL

Arabs in Israel. Jerusalem, Ministry for Foreign Affairs, 1961.

Ben-Gurion, D., Rebirth and Destiny of Israel. New York, Philosophical Library, 1954.
Israel: Years of Challenge. New York, Holt, Rinehart and Winston, 1963.

Bentwich, N., Israel Resurgent. London, Benn, 1960.
The New Old Land of Israel. London, Allen, 1960.

Elston, D.R., Israel, The Making of a Nation. London, Oxford University Press, 1963.

Hausner, G., Justice in Jerusalem. New York, Harper, 1966.

Israel Today Pamphlets. A series published by The Jewish Agency for Israel. Jerusalem.

Morris, Y., Masters of the Desert: 6,000 Years in the Negev. New York, Putnam, 1961.

Pearlman, M., The Capture and Trial of Adolf Eichmann. New York, Simon and Schuster, 1963.

Stevenson, W., Strike Zion. New York, Bantam Books, 1967.

Weiner, H., The Wild Goats of Ein Gedi (religious and philosophical trends). New York, Doubleday, 1961.

BIOGRAPHY

Bein, A., Theodore Herzl. Philadelphia, Jewish Publications Society, 1941.

Litvinoff, B., Story of David Ben-Gurion. Dobbs Ferry, N. Y., Oceana Publications, 1960.

Syrkin, M., The Way of Valor: A Biography of Golda Myerson (Meir). New York, Sharon, 1955.

Weizmann, Ch., Trial and Error (autobiography). London, Hamilton, 1940.

CULTURAL ACTIVITIES

Albright, W. J., The Archaeology of Palestine. Harmondsworth, Penguin Books, 1960.

Halkin, S., Modern Hebrew Literature. New York, Schocken, 1950.

Pearlman, M., Historical Sites in Israel.

Yadin, Y., The Message of the Scrolls. New York, Simon and Schuster, 1957.

Yadin, Y., Masada. New York, Random House, 1966.

ECONOMIC AND SOCIAL

Baratz, J., Village by the Jordan. London, The Harvill Press, 1954.

Bein, A., Return to the Soil. Jerusalem, Zionist Organization, 1952.

Cohen, S. B., Arab Villages in Israel.

Darin-Drabkin, H., Patterns of Cooperative Agriculture in Israel. Tel Aviv, Israel Institute for Books, 1962.

Guide to the Kibbutz. Tel Aviv, Ichud Habonim, 1963.

Malkosh, N., Co-operation in Israel. Tel Aviv, Histadrut, 1961.

Orni, E., Forms of Settlement. Jerusalem, Zionist Organization, 1960.

Spiro, M. E., Kibbutz—Venture in Utopia. Cambridge, Mass., Harvard University Press, 1956.
Children of the Kibbutz. Cambridge, Mass., Harvard University Press, 1958.

HISTORICAL

Cohen, I., A Short History of Zionism. London, Muller, 1951.

Epstein, I., Judaism, A Historical Presentation. Harmondsworth, Penguin, 1959.

Eytan, W., The First Ten Years. A Diplomatic History of Israel. New York, Simon and Schuster, 1958.

Granados, G. J., The Birth of Israel. New York, Knopf, 1948.

Henriques, R., One Hundred Hours to Suez. New York, Viking Press. 1957.

Levin, H., Jerusalem Embattled. London, Gollancz, 1950.

Lorch, N., The Edge of the Sword: Israel's War of Independence 1947-1949. London, Putnam, 1961.

MacDonald, J., My Mission in Israel. New York, Simon and Schuster, 1951.

Parkes, J., A History of the Jewish People. London, Weidenfeld and Nicolson, 1962.
A History of Palestine From 135 A.D. to Modern Times. London, Gollancz, 1949.

Sharef, Zeev, Three Days (birth of Israel). London, Allen, 1962.

Sykes, C., Crossroads to Israel.

Terrien, S., The Golden Bible Atlas. New York, Golden Press, 1957.

LAW AND GOVERNMENT

Baker, H. E., The Legal System of Israel. London, Sweet and Maxwell, 1961.

Rosenne, S., the Constitutional and Legal System of Israel, New York, Israel Office of Information, 1957.

Asterisks (*) denote pages on which the subjects are illustrated or discussed in captions.

159

Illustration Credits

All photographs are by Werner Braun, with the exception of those on the following pages:

48: Hebrew University, New York
50, 54 top left, 59, 61 bottom right, 69: Israel Tourist Office, Tel Aviv
54 top right: Israel Museum, Jerusalem
64 left, 103, 104, 107, 142 right, 143, 144, 146, 148 left, 149 left, 151: Jordanian Tourist Office, New York
90: Bibliothèque Nationale, Paris
82 left, 102, 105, 108, 109, 114 right, 148 right, 149 right, 152, 155: Epoca
106: Wide World

Charts and maps: pp. 10, 55, 56, 57: Golden Press
14-15: Société française d'études et de réalisations cartographiques (S.F.E.R.C.)
13, 92-93: Société graphique et cartographique